GET THE MOST FROM YOUR CLOTHES

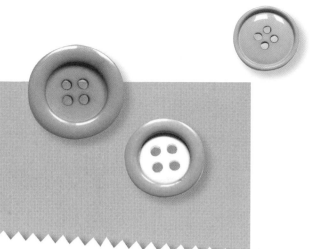

GET THE
MOST
FROM YOUR
CLOTHES

Marion Elliot

D&C
David and Charles
www.rucraft.co.uk

For Neil and Stella.

A DAVID & CHARLES BOOK
Copyright © David & Charles Limited 2011

David & Charles is an F+W Media Inc. company
4700 East Galbraith Road, Cincinnati, OH 45236

First published in the UK and US in 2011

Text and designs copyright © Marion Elliot 2011

All photography by Lorna Yabsley except:
Page 31 (bottom left) © Pretty Rubbish (www.prettyrubbish.org)
Page 31 (right) © Mandy Shaw (www.dandeliondesigns.co.uk)
Page 90 (bottom right) © iStockphoto (www.istockphoto.com)
Page 122 (bottom) © The Make Lounge (www.themakelounge.com)

With special thanks to Boden (www.boden.co.uk) for allowing us to include an image of their lovely dress, show on page 60 (top right)

A catalogue record for this book is available from the British Library.

ISBN-13: 978-0-7153-3842-1 paperback
ISBN-10: 0-7153-3842-0 paperback

Printed in China by RR Donnelley
for David & Charles
Brunel House, Newton Abbot, Devon

Publisher Alison Myer
Acquisitions Editor Jennifer Fox-Proverbs
Editor James Brooks
Project Editor Jo Richardson
Senior Designer Mia Trenoweth
Photographer Lorna Yabsley
Production Controller Kelly Smith
Pre Press Natasha Jorden and Jodie Culpin

David and Charles publish high-quality books on a wide range of subjects.
For more great book ideas visit: www.rucraft.co.uk

GET THE MOST FROM...

GET THE MOST!

Hold it right there! Put down those new clothes and move away from the checkout. Go home, take a long, hard look at the contents of your wardrobe and think upcycling, revamping and glamorizing instead of reaching for your plastic. For no matter how tired your clothes seem to you right now, you can be certain that, with a little TLC, you can transform them into desirable must-haves without spending a penny.

If you've ever searched through your wardrobe on the morning of a big night out and thought 'Help, I've got nothing to wear!', then help is indeed at hand. This book will show you all sorts of nifty tricks and tips for transforming your clothes into visions of loveliness, by enhancing what's hot and minimizing what's not. You may already be a bit of a whizz on the sewing machine. If so, there are heaps of ideas for nips, tucks and pleats to reshape and restyle sad and saggy old outfits. But should altering and upcycling clothes be uncharted territory for you, then you'll find plenty here to fire your imagination and enhance your skills. There are loads of quick fixes too, if there's just no time to thread up your machine. Once you start to experiment and discover the potential, you'll be hooked on making over your entire wardrobe!

The sad truth is that we have all become spoiled by the ready availability of clothes so cheap that we can afford to buy a new wardrobe every season. When they wear out or we grow tired of them, we simply chuck them away. We tend not to dwell on how clothes could possibly cost so little, who makes them and how much they're paid, or how the raw materials to make them are produced. The time has come for us to re-evaluate the way that we consume the world's resources.

Happily, there has been a shift in attitude, and now there are all sorts of opportunities to make do and mend in the spirit of our forebears, who knew how to get the most from their clothes while looking impeccably turned out. The rise of upcycling clothes and fabrics into fantastic new creations is cool once more, and what was once the preserve of high-end boutiques is becoming mainstream. There are all sorts of great initiatives to swap or 'swish' clothes you no longer want, allowing you to get your hands on great garments at zero cost. The internet is awash with great clothes-swap sites, and it has never been more hip to wear vintage.

So now grab those cast-offs and breathe new life into them, instead of buying yet more stuff you really don't need – you know it makes sense!

GET THE MOST FROM...

Your CLOTHES

Cardi Creative

Got an ageing, tired, but much-loved cardigan that's too precious to part with? With a speedy recut and a swift bit of ruffling, you can restyle it into a fab and flattering bolero cardi that's totally on trend. You don't even need to felt your woolly first, unless it's absolutely huge – just wash, dry and press it, and you're ready to roll!

Get into it...

Do you need a shrink?

Choose a cardi with a bit of body to it. If it's too thin, it won't support the weight of the ruffled trim and will bag and sag once the trim is attached – not a good look! To improve the density of the knit and make it more like felt, a speedy shrink could be the answer. Look at the label to check the wool content, and if it's 90% or above, then it's the ideal candidate for a quick whizz through the hot cycle. However, if it's already a snug fit, don't be tempted in case you shrink it too much – it's an irreversible process and I've lost many a fab garment to a moment of hot-water madness!

What's your fibre?

As it's not essential to felt your cardi, you can choose one made from any yarn you like. Synthetics and synthetic mixes like nylon and Lycra® are soft and easy to sew, yet have enough body to make beautiful ruffles. They also have the added bonus of being non-fray, so you don't need to worry about finishing fiddly edges before you attach your ruffles. Don't be afraid to mix and match different fibres either. Stretchy fabrics with metallic fibres such as lurex make stunning contrasting trims for plain boleros. Just remember that as long as they can all be washed at the same temperature, you can try out all sorts of interesting fabric combinations. If you're in any doubt, once your cardi is restyled, simply hand wash it for a safe outcome.

Just cut it out

The beauty of this design is its versatility. Boleros come in lots of different styles, from slinky little shrugs to waist-length jackets, so you're bound to find a fit and length that suits your personal style. And one of the main joys of making a bolero is that it's really simple! When you've decided on your basic design, you just need to summon up the courage to chop your cardi into shape. Be brave, because it's just like cutting a shape out of a piece of paper. If you haven't felted the fabric, you'll need to stay stitch the raw edges of your cardi after you've reshaped the front, to stop it from fraying (see Step 3). If you have, then your snazzy new bolero is ready for its decadent trimming!

If you decide to felt your cardi, turn to the Nifty Knits feature for some practical tips on how to achieve the best results.

Place a sheet of newspaper inside your cardi before you draw around your pattern onto the front. This will prevent the ink from bleeding through from the front to the back.

Get it together...

* Old woollen cardigan and matching thread
* Contrasting sweater and matching thread
* Newspaper
* Marker pen
* Scissors
* Sewing machine with needle for knitted fabrics
* 1m (1¼yd) broad satin ribbon in colour to match ruffle edging
* Iron
* Pins
* Hand sewing needle
* Shirring elastic

1 Place your cardigan flat on your work surface. Make a template out of newspaper of the front of the cardigan, then draw a curved edge from the neckline to the side of the template and cut it out to make a pattern. Place the pattern on each side of the cardigan and draw around it, flipping it over so that you can use it on both the left and right sides of the cardigan.

2 Cut away the excess cardigan where marked to make your bolero shape. Trim the sleeves to three-quarter length. Make sure they are both the same length by cutting one, then folding the cardigan in half with one sleeve on top of another and trimming the second to match.

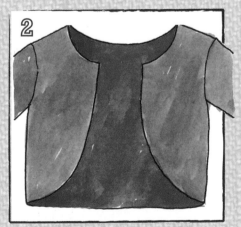

Use a sewing machine needle for knitted fabrics when stay stitching around your bolero. This type of needle has a ballpoint that slips easily through the fibres without splitting them, giving a flat, neat seam.

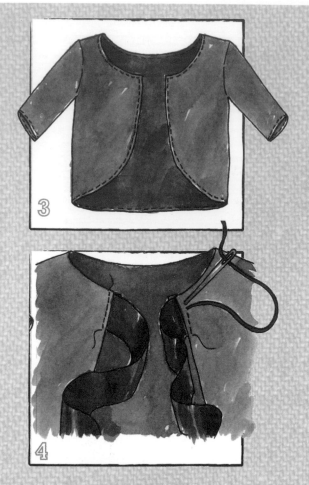

3 Set your sewing machine to the longest straight stitch and insert a ballpoint needle for knitted fabrics. Sew all the way around the edge of the bolero to keep the fabric from stretching or fraying.

4 Cut two 50cm (20in) lengths of broad satin ribbon. Press under the raw edge at the top of each piece, then pin and hand stitch them with matching thread at the neck of the bolero to make ties.

5 To make the ruffled edging, place your contrasting woolly flat on your work surface and cut it into as many 3cm- (1¼in-) wide strips as possible. Pin and machine stitch the strips together to make one long band.

6 Wind shirring elastic onto an empty bobbin and place it in your sewing machine. Using matching thread and a fairly long stitch, sew slowly down the centre of the contrasting band to ruffle it.

7 Pin the ruffled edging around your bolero and sleeves, aligning the centre of the ruffle with the edge of the bolero. Using matching thread, hand stitch the edging in place on the back of the bolero.

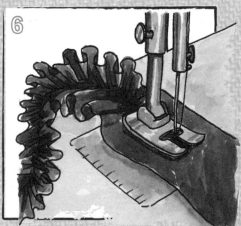

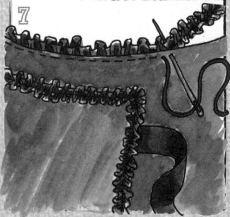

Get more...

» Found two cardies you really like?
For an **instant makeover**, try **swapping the sleeves** – this looks really cool with two strongly contrasting colours.

• If you're feeling particularly adventurous, why not go for a **two-** or even **three-colourway combo** – see photo right.

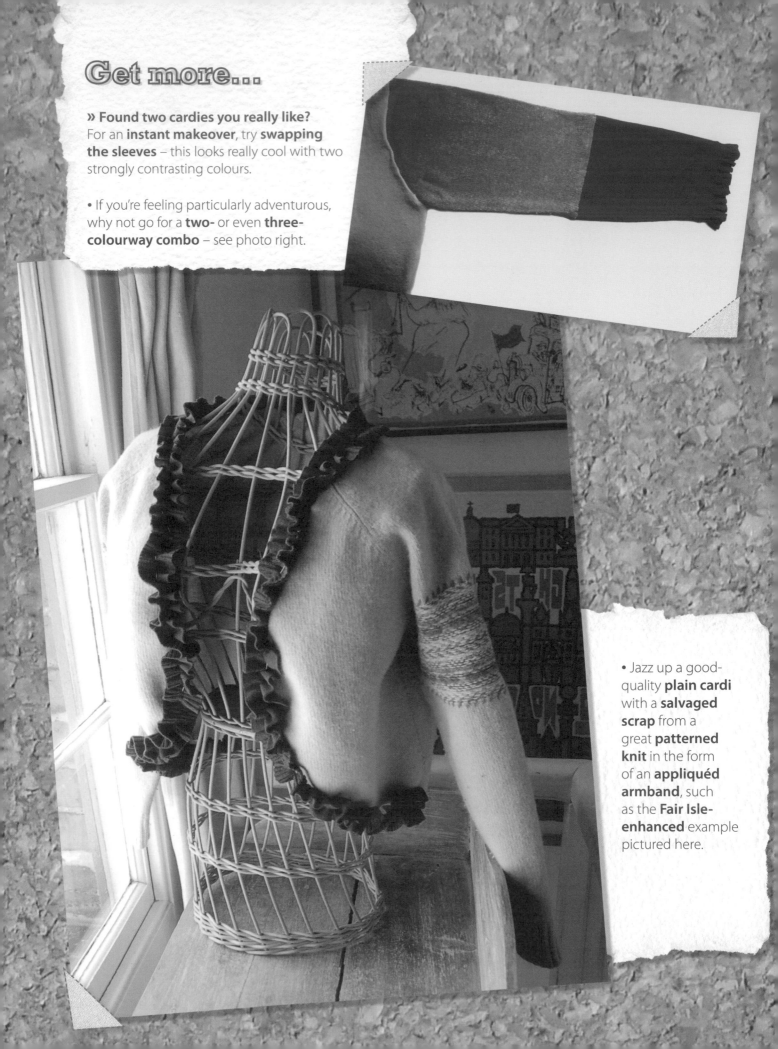

• Jazz up a good-quality **plain cardi** with a **salvaged scrap** from a great **patterned knit** in the form of an **appliquéd armband**, such as the **Fair Isle-enhanced** example pictured here.

» **Found a great cardi, but it's just too big?** If it's pure wool, or has only a very small percentage of manmade fibres, think about felting it before you begin (see the Nifty Knits feature). This will produce a much tighter, denser fabric and could reduce the size of your cardi by as much as half. But keep an eye on it in the wash, and don't get too carried away with the tumble dryer!

» **Want to make an untrimmed bolero?**
Simply **machine stitch** around the **raw edges** of your cardi with a **medium-length zigzag stitch**. This will neaten the edges and prevent them from fraying, and will also give them an **attractive wavy** appearance.

» **Can't get hold of any shirring elastic?** Cut **strips** of **contrasting fabric** from an **old sweater** as before, then set your **sewing machine** to the **longest stitch** and sew along the **centre** of the strips, without securing the thread at the end. **Pull up** the thread to **ruffle** the fabric by hand, and stitch to your bolero as before.

» **Fancy a different sort of trimming?** Instead of using a ruffled edging to trim your bolero:

• edge with flat, narrow **contrasting satin ribbon** for a really **cool, retro look** – think Grace Kelly and little Chanel jackets

• use **sequins, little beads, mini bobble trim** or **small buttons** for a completely different approach

Before you recut your cardi, you'll need to remove all the buttons, but don't discard them, as they'll come in handy for other projects.

» **Need some practice to find your perfect style?** Cut out **prototype bolero shapes** from **old T-shirts** before chopping up your favourite cardi – once you've found a style you like, you can use the tee as a **template** for the real thing.

Puffball Revival

I spotted a floral wrapover dress in a charity shop whose Eastern-style fabric I just loved. I knew it would be very easy to salvage a skirt from its generous proportions, so I planned to simply remove the bodice and shorten the dress to make a straightforward, on the knee number. But I then found a feature on puffball minis in a magazine and knew it was the perfect treatment.

Get into it...

Waist not
Analyse your dress carefully before you buy it, to see what features you can salvage for your new skirt. The one I chose had a wide tie belt that fastened at the back (see photo left), which was perfect for keeping the skirt in place at the waist once the bodice was removed. This was a real time-saver, as otherwise I would have needed to make a new waistband in order to gather up the top edge of the skirt and give it a neat finish.

Keep it natural
I always look for clothes in natural fabrics like cotton and linen when I'm on the prowl, because I find them so much easier to handle than synthetics. I am prepared to make exceptions for really amazing fabrics, but none of us want to machine sew slippery, slidey satins and nylons.

For more insider hints and tips on how to select the right candidates for upcycling, see the Makeover Magic feature.

Pump it up
I chose this dress to upcycle into a puffball skirt because it's cut on the bias, which means that it's cut diagonally to the weave of the fabric rather than on the straight. When a garment is cut in this way, it folds and drapes very fluidly as well as yielding far more fabric. I knew that the skirt section would gather and puff up beautifully, as there was an ample amount of fabric to play with, so I decided on a gently gathered style.

Quick fix
Once I'd removed the bodice from the skirt, I was left with a very long dress zip, which I unpicked (and carefully put aside for later use, of course). To save inserting another zip, I simply machine stitched the side seam to within 5cm (2in) of the waistband. Then I added a press stud (snap fastener) at the top, which I knew would be hidden by the ties when they were tied around the waist at the back.

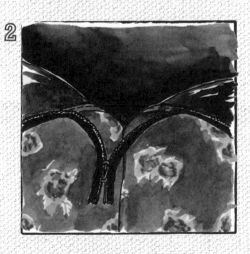

1 Place the dress on a flat surface and carefully unpick the bodice section. Press under the raw edge at the top of the skirt and machine stitch in place.

2 Remove the zip from the side of the dress. Pin the sides of the dress together and machine stitch to within 5cm (2in) of the waistband. Add a press stud (snap fastener) to the waistband.

3 Decide on the length of your skirt. Measure and trim the skirt section of the dress to this length, allowing a narrow turning of the raw edge and 3cm (1¼in) for a casing for the elastic. Press under the raw edge and then the turning for the casing, pin and machine stitch in place, leaving a 3cm (1¼in) gap in the casing to insert the elastic.

4 Cut a length of elastic to fit around the lower edge of the skirt. Insert one end of the elastic into the casing and machine stitch it to keep it in place. Attach the other end to a small safety pin and thread it through the casing. Pull the elastic to the desired tension, then trim and machine stitch the free end in place.

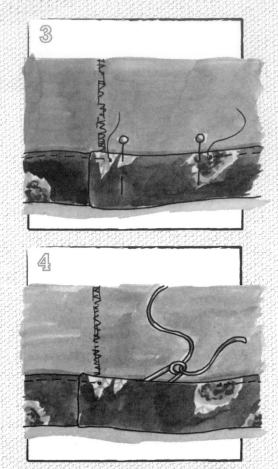

Get more...

» A puffball-style mini skirt really isn't your thing? Simply press under a 1.5cm (⅝in) turning at the bottom of your skirt and machine stitch the hem in place. If you've found a decent bias-cut dress, there will still be enough fabric available to make a lovely full skirt.

» I used very narrow hat elastic to pull in the lower edge of my skirt. This type of elastic is round, not flat, so rolls nicely without turning over. Because of its width, it makes very gentle, loose gathers that drape and flow fluidly at the lower edge of the skirt.

» There are lots of ways to customize your skirt still further:

• Add a **bow** made from leftover fabric, or a length of **wide satin ribbon** to the **waistband** (see photo right).

• If your original dress has **patch pockets**, don't remove them but incorporate into your skirt for a **relaxed style**.

• If you go for the **ungathered option**, add a touch of **retro chic** with a row of **mini bobble fringe**, **lace** or **narrow velvet ribbon** along the lower edge (see photo below).

» The **puffball look** is so easy to achieve and versatile that you can use it to groove up the hems of **cardigans**, **blouses**, **trousers** and others kinds of garment. One of the most effective applications I've seen was a thin, **silver neoprene jacket** with a **gathered hem** – it looked fantastic in metallic fabric and made a super-stylish fashion statement.

Flicking through fashion magazines is a great way to spark off ideas for transforming tired but pretty frocks and other outdated garments into on-trend items.

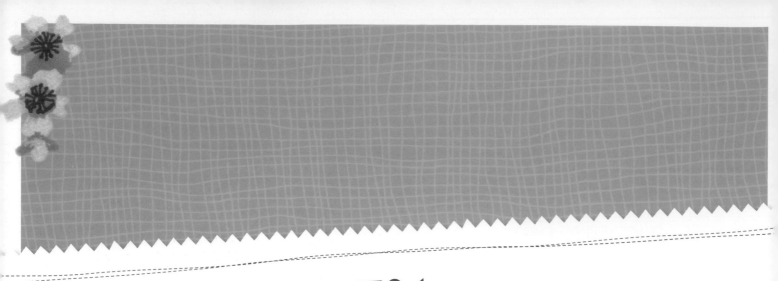

Tailor Fit

Take a good look at the men's jackets in charity shops or thrift stores, as sometimes you'll find really good-quality examples like this one, made from expensive cloth and with hand tailoring on the reveres. But don't be put off by their vast size and dull appearance. With a few basic tailoring tricks, you can achieve the right fit and then use all sorts of decorative techniques to jazz them up.

Get into it...

Quality counts

Always choose a standout, high-quality garment when you're embarking on a project like this. You'll be investing precious time and materials, so don't waste them on an inferior item. Quality doesn't necessarily equal expense. I picked this jacket up for very little money, but I've had enough experience of rummaging around in charity shops to recognize an impressive garment when I see it. Check clothing labels and pick out good brands if possible, or go for quality vintage items. A jacket made from cloth with a very high wool content is promising too, so always read the care label for clues.

Chalk it up

Sometimes you'll need to make markings on your jacket to indicate the size and position of things like cutting lines and darts. Traditionally in the tailoring industry, tailor's chalk is used to mark up fabric with lines that can simply be brushed or washed out afterwards. Tailor's chalk is triangular in shape, and is very soft and easy to use. It generally comes in white or yellow, so is perfect for making highly visible markings on dark suiting.

Dart about

Most men's jackets will be shaped at the front with slim darts to take in the fullness of the fabric and draw in the waist slightly. Although the original darts won't go in nearly far enough to fit a woman, it's easy to adjust them to fit a female figure with a slimmer ribcage and waist. To remake the darts, simply unpick the lining from the lower edge of the jacket so that you can get to the darts. Use tailor's chalk to draw a new line to the required width alongside the existing darts, then machine stitch along the chalk line to create a more generous dart.

Arm's length

The sleeves of men's jackets are often far too long. The easiest way to deal with this is simply to turn them up and slip stitch to the required length. But for a more decorative effect, cut off the excess sleeve to the right length, less about 5cm (2in), then trim the raw edges with a border of contrasting fabric. You could also trim with bias binding or satin ribbon, in which case trim the sleeves to exactly the right length first.

What to know more about using darts and reshaping? See the Fabulous Fitting feature.

- Jacket and matching thread
- Seam ripper
- Tailor's chalk and ruler
- Scissors
- Pins
- Sewing machine
- Iron
- Hand sewing needle
- Dress fabric with printed motifs and matching thread
- Fusible webbing
- Scraps of contrasting fabric and matching thread
- Oversize snap fastener (optional)
- Coordinating fabric-covered button (optional)

1 Remove any buttons from the jacket (save for future use). Put on the jacket and find your natural waistline. Unpick the lining, using a seam ripper, as far as the waist, then use tailor's chalk and a ruler to mark a line across the back and front of the jacket at waist length. Cut across the line to separate the upper and lower halves of the jacket.

2 On the inside of the upper jacket, mark the position of the bust darts. Pin and machine stitch them in place, then press flat.

3 Once the darts are in place, pin and tack (baste) the upper and lower halves of the jacket together again, folding the fabric in the lower half where necessary to ease in the fullness.

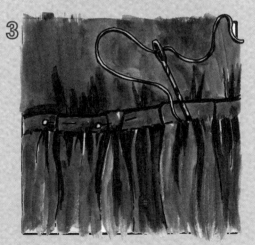

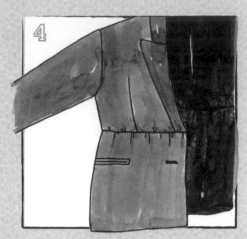

4 Machine stitch the two halves of the jacket together again, then press the seams flat.

5 To make the appliquéd decorations, choose the motifs you want to use from your printed dress fabric and apply fusible webbing to the backs. Cut the motifs out.

6 Remove the backing paper and position your motifs right side up on the jacket. Iron them to the jacket, then machine stitch roughly around the edges to appliqué them in place.

7 Decide how long you want your jacket sleeves to be and mark the new length with tailor's chalk. Cut off the excess fabric.

8 Cut two bands of contrasting fabric 15cm (6in) deep, and long enough to fit around the end of each sleeve. Pin the bands around the sleeves, with right sides facing. Machine stitch in place, then pin the edges of each band together and seam these too.

9 Press the seams open on the wrong side of the fabric, then press under a 1.5cm (⅝in) seam along the raw edge of each band. Press the turned edges of the bands under and slip stitch in place on the inside of the sleeves.

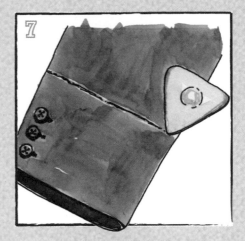

To add an eye-catching fastening

Recutting the jacket may well deprive you of functioning buttonholes. If this is the case, simply add a closure with an oversize snap fastener (the larger the popper, the groovier they look) where the button and buttonhole would normally go. Then sew a large button to the front of the jacket, directly over the popper. If you can't find a button you like, try making an original using a fabric-covered button – see the Cool Customizing feature, or create with a covered-button kit.

Get more...

» Tucks are a simple way of gathering in excess fullness in a garment. To make a tuck, fold over and press the fabric, then stitch along the top edge to keep the fabric flat. It's a much neater way of reducing the fabric than gathering, which is quite difficult to do successfully with a heavy garment like a jacket.

» You can give a jacket a radical new look by:

• **cutting a curved edge** into the **front or back**; **removing** the **front** as far as the **waist** and leaving the **back intact**; **removing** the **front** and **back** completely just **below the waistline**

• **cutting sleeves** to **bracelet** or **elbow** length; **removing** the **sleeves** altogether.

For the best results, cut a paper pattern for the new shape and unpick the lining before you do any cutting.

» You can mix and match two or more jackets to great effect by:

• **choosing** two **wildly contrasting fabrics**, then **swapping sleeves**, **reveres** and **pockets** for ultra-funky results

• **combining** the **top half** of a **jacket** with the **bottom half** of a **cardi**, or the **sleeves** of a **sweater** with the **body** of a **jacket**

» Lots of jackets come with dull, self-coloured **buttons** that don't do a lot for the overall effect. A very quick and easy makeover is to **replace** the boring originals with **fabric-covered alternatives**, customized with the fabric of your choice. You will need a covered-button kit to make these, which you'll find in craft supplies shops or online (see photos above and left).

» Nothing perks up a jacket more quickly than a **new lining** – see the one pictured right. A flash of **bright satin** makes even the most mundane jacket effortlessly stylish, and it's not hard to replace the original lining. First unpick the old lining, then open all the seams and press them flat. Use these as pattern pieces to cut a new lining, machine stitch together and insert and attach to the jacket.

Many young and established textile designers are embracing sustainability and upcycling clothes to make dynamic pieces, such as the one pictured here. So check out their designs online, to buy and/or for inspiration (see Suppliers).

» Fancy stitching can give your jacket a speedy facelift:

• Add a **few rows** of **rustic embroidery** in **bright woollen yarn**.

• Add lines of simple standards like **chain stitch**, **cross stitch** or **herringbone stitch** around the **cuffs** and **hem**.

• **Trace** off **simple motifs** from your **favourite fabric**, then transfer to your jacket and work in **split** or c**hain stitch**. **Hearts** and **stars** look especially good, and add a **folk art** feel.

» Another good look is to **insert** an **open-ended zip** (salvaged from an old cardi, naturally!) at the **jacket opening**. You can always adjust the darts at the front and back, if necessary.

Trendy Tricolour

This groovy girl's dress is upcycled from three different garments, all outgrown or in need of TLC. I found a long-sleeved tee in a colour that went beautifully with an old cardi of my daughter's, so I stitched a section to the cardi bottom, then made an obi-style tie from a pair of cotton jersey tights (pantyhose) to cinch the dress in at the waist. A salvaged set of oversize buttons provided the perfect finishing touch.

Get into it...

In for a stretch

Cotton jersey fabric is a stretch knit that can be successfully sewn on your machine if you use the appropriate needles. You'll need ballpoint machine needles in the right gauge for your fabric (70 for fine, 80 for medium-weight or 90 for heavyweight knits) and polyester cotton.

It'll all come out in the wash...

Consider the weight of the fabrics you are combining before going ahead. For example, a very thick cardi and a flimsy T-shirt will not work well together, because the weight of one will distort the shape of the other. The aim is to combine similar garments so that they look and feel as if they're made for each other. The cardi, tee and tights I used here are all made from cotton jersey, so all washable at the same temperature. I made sure that the ribbon and sequins could be laundered too, so that all the 'ingredients' could be confidently combined.

Loosen up

Once a cardi gets too small, it's often tight across the chest and under the arms, but fits fine elsewhere. If yours is too tight, carefully unpick the sleeves and remove them to leave a bodice. Then cut the armholes of the bodice slightly larger, and insert a new pair of sleeves from a larger sweater or cardi to make it extra roomy.

In the bag

Once I'd cut the legs off the tights (pantyhose) to make the obi tie, I was left with a pair of 'shorts' that I knew would make a great little bag. I stitched them across, just above the gusset, and trimmed the excess, then added a long strap made from a fake pony-skin belt. For extra bling, I added a bow tied from a strip of leftover tee and a sequin trim.

Get it together...

* Old cotton jersey cardigan and matching thread
* Old cotton jersey T-shirt and matching thread
* Pair of cotton jersey tights (pantyhose) and matching thread
* Iron
* Pins
* Sewing machine
* Scissors
* 4 contrasting buttons with strong matching thread
* Hand sewing needle
* 50cm (20in) broad ribbon in a coordinating colour (optional)
* 1m (1¼yd) strung sequins for dress and bag (optional)
* Narrow leather belt (for optional bag)

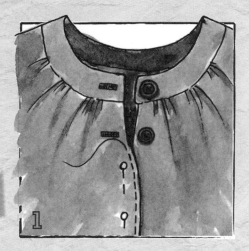

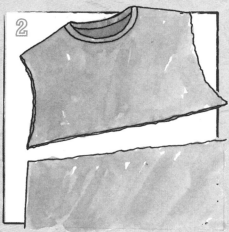

1 Press the cardigan completely flat. Fasten the buttons, then pin the front opening together, overlapping the edges accurately and neatly. Using your sewing machine, topstitch the opening closed from just below the buttons.

2 For the skirt section, cut off the sleeves and the top section of the T-shirt, just below the armholes. Overstitch the raw edge of the T-shirt using a narrow zigzag stitch on your sewing machine and matching thread.

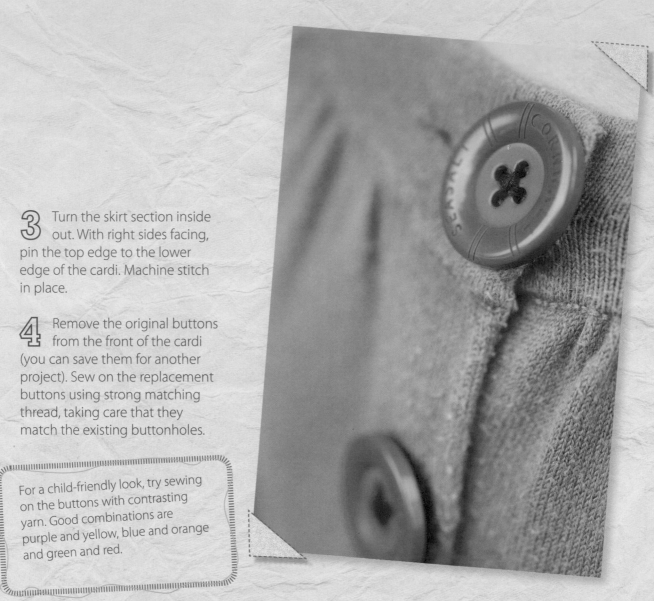

3 Turn the skirt section inside out. With right sides facing, pin the top edge to the lower edge of the cardi. Machine stitch in place.

4 Remove the original buttons from the front of the cardi (you can save them for another project). Sew on the replacement buttons using strong matching thread, taking care that they match the existing buttonholes.

For a child-friendly look, try sewing on the buttons with contrasting yarn. Good combinations are purple and yellow, blue and orange and green and red.

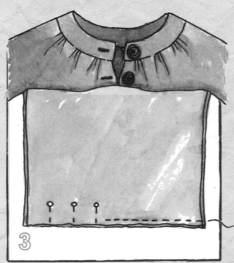

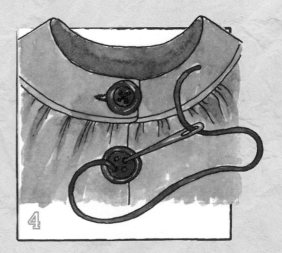

5 Cut the legs off the pair of tights (pantyhose) just below the gusset. Fold one of the legs in half and cut it into two equal sections.

6 To make the obi tie, turn the two half sections of leg inside out. With right sides facing, pin the top edge of each half to the ends of the uncut leg. Machine stitch together, then turn right side out again.

7 Cut the ends of the obi tie diagonally to neaten them. Overstitch the raw edges with narrow zigzag stitch on your sewing machine to stop them fraying.

8 Fold the obi tie in half and press it to find the midpoint. Pin the belt to the front of the dress, over the join between the top and skirt, with the middle of the belt in the centre of the dress. Topstitch slowly along the upper and lower edges of the belt to attach it to the dress, leaving the excess tie ends for tying.

Track down some really brightly coloured tights (pantyhose) if you can – they look great against flat, plain colours.

To trim with ribbon and sequins

The ribbon can be hand stitched around the waist, or you can use a machine if yours has a free arm that you can insert inside the garment to separate the layers. The sequins can either be hand stitched or attached with high-tack fabric glue, which is washable but the sequins will eventually wear loose.

Get more...

» Don't stop at cardies when it comes to creating a frock. You can make fab little summer dresses by taking **two** of a girl's **favourite old T-shirts** and **splicing them together**:

• For the skirt, cut the top section off one, just below the sleeves, and discard the sleeves. Stitch the skirt to the lower edge of the other T-shirt.

• Use really wild pattern and colour combinations for the coolest look.

• Then use the same recipe to whip yourself up a lovely little summer smock from two of your old tees in no time at all!

» **No suitable tights (pantyhose) to hand?** Just cut off the **ribbed section** from the lower edge of a **large sweater** or **cardigan** and use this instead. Simply **overstitch** the raw edge with a row of **narrow zigzags** on your sewing machine before you start, unless the woolly has been felted in the washing machine first, to prevent it fraying.

» **Fancy a dress with a fuller skirt?** Look for an XXL T-shirt, which will give you much more fabric to work with. You can then gather the top edge of the skirt section before you stitch it to the cardi. To gather the tee:

• either sew a row of shirring elastic along the top edge on your sewing machine, or

• make a line of tacking (basting) stitches without fastening the thread at the end and pull the thread up, adjusting the fabric to fit around the lower edge of the cardi.

» You can use your sewing machine to stitch the leather belt strap to your bag, as long as you use the right needle. Get hold of some **leather needles**, which have very sharp points that cut through the leather like blades. Use **polyester thread** and a **medium to long stitch**, and **sew very slowly** so that you don't break the needle.

If you're looking for more exciting ideas about creative things you can do with old woollies, including instructions on how to felt them, see the Nifty Knits feature.

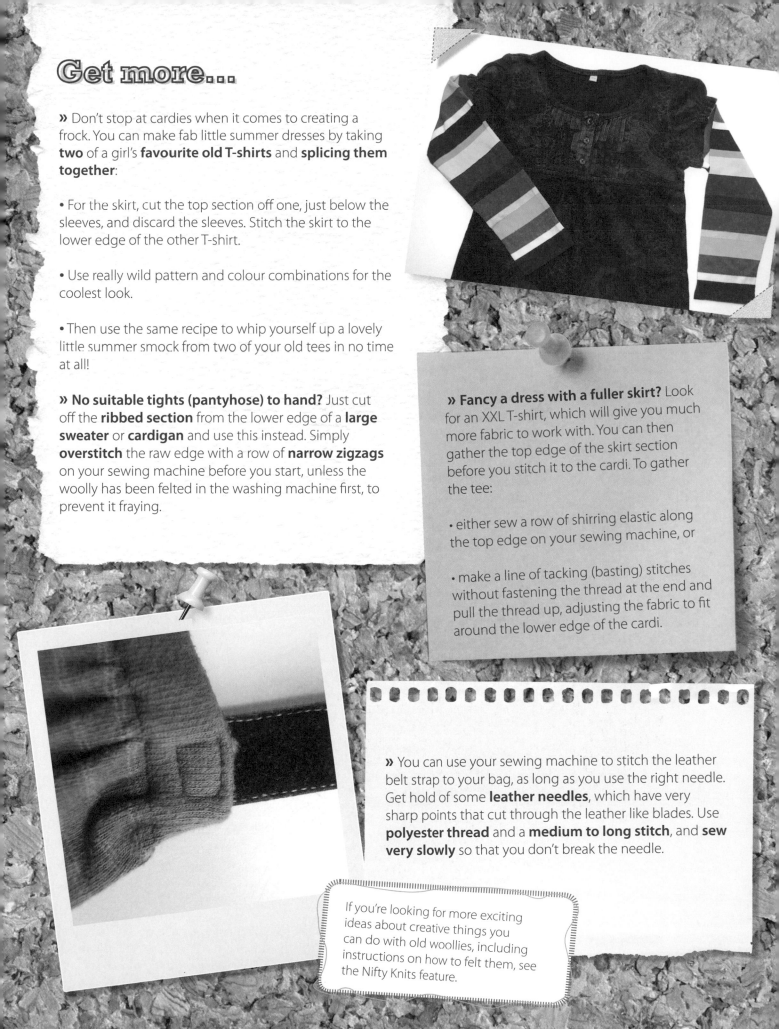

Top Tees

Who would guess that these two fantastic halter-neck tops took less than an hour to make? What's more, they were created from a couple of humble but huge T-shirts that were well past their sell-by dates. They can be dressed up or down according to your mood, so are great for everyday wear or just as cool for an evening out with friends.

Get into it...

Mix 'n' match

Big tees are perfect for upcycling, and the larger and baggier the better (I used men's XXL), as you get loads of fabric to play around with. Try to find pairs of T-shirts that work well together colourwise, such as the duck egg blue and chocolate brown ones here. This way, you can use scraps from each to embellish the other, as I have done, adding a patch pocket with a floral motif to one and combining the two colours into a pretty rosette corsage for the other.

Well drawn

Halter tops are one of those wardrobe staples that always looks good. I've found that gathering up the fabric on a drawstring, as here, creates a lovely ruched effect that flatters everyone, and with so much fabric in the T-shirt, you get a lovely draped effect when you gather in the neckline. The fullness of the tees means that the lower edge flares out when the top half is gathered in, giving a very on-trend, A-line shape.

Sew like a pro

T-shirts are generally made from knitted cotton, or cotton-mix jersey fabric. The softness of the cotton jersey fabric means that it drapes beautifully and is very easy to reshape. But don't be put off it by fears of how to sew – it's surprisingly easy if you have the right needles. You'll need a ballpoint sewing machine needle to stitch jersey fabric, as an ordinary needle is too sharp and will pucker up the fabric, spoiling the finish. This is the same kind of needle you need for felted wool and any knitted or stretch fabric. Practise your machine stitching on off-cuts of holey old T-shirts before you embark on a project. You don't need to change the machine tension or use special cotton, and once you get used to the sensation of sewing a stretchy fabric, you'll learn how to handle it like a pro.

> Needles are not expensive, so it's worth getting a pack of mixed-gauge ballpoint ones for your machine ready to makeover any knitted or stretch fabric garments.

Clever cutting

When you cut out things like the pocket on the front of the brown halter top, look for ways to save time by incorporating existing features. For example, I placed the top edge of the pocket pattern along the lower, hemmed edge of the sleeve section I'd removed earlier. This ensured that my pocket already had a finished top edge, saving me the effort of hemming it.

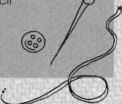

Get it together...

- Two men's XXL T-shirts in contrasting colours and matching thread
- Scissors
- Ruler and fine marker pen
- Sewing machine
- Narrow ribbon
- Safety pin
- Hat elastic
- Hand sewing needle
- Tracing paper and pencil
- Thin paper
- 2 contrasting buttons

1 Place the T-shirt for the pocket treatment on a flat surface. Carefully trim away the sleeves at either side of the tee. Put them to one side, as you'll need them later.

2 Find the lowest point of the T-shirt neckline. Draw a straight line across the front of the T-shirt, about 1cm (⅜in) below this point. Cut off the neck section from the front and back of the T-shirt, along the line.

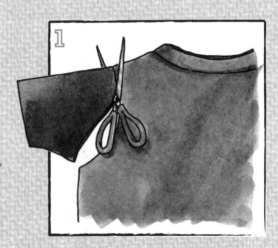

3 Turn the T-shirt over. On the back of the shirt, draw a straight line across the shirt, about 3cm (1¼in) up from the bottom of the armhole curve. Cut away the excess fabric along this line.

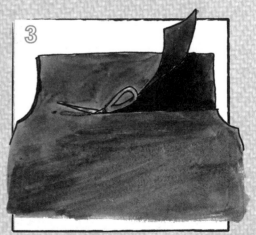

4 Press under a 1cm (⅜in) hem around the armholes, from the top of the T-shirt front to the top edge of the back. Machine stitch the hems in place.

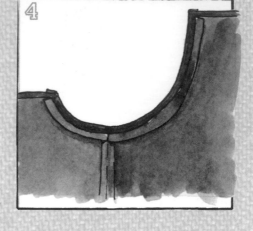

5 Press under a 4cm (1½in) turning at the front of the T-shirt. Machine stitch the turning in place, about 1cm (⅜in) from the lower edge. To make the casing for the halter ribbon tie, machine stitch along the turning again, but this time about 1.5cm (⅝in) from the upper edge.

6 Press under a 1.5cm (⅝in) turning along the top of the T-shirt back to make a casing for the elastic. Machine stitch in place.

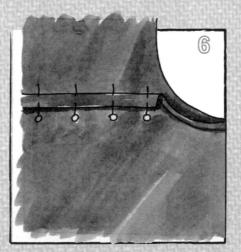

7 Cut a long length of narrow ribbon for the halter tie. Attach one end to a safety pin and pass it through the casing on the front of the top. Pull the ribbon through the casing to give an equal amount at either side.

8 Cut a long length of hat elastic to gather in the back of the halter top. Attach one end to the safety pin and pass it through the casing on the back. Pull the elastic through the casing and then pull up to the desired fullness. Trim off the excess and firmly hand stitch the ends of the elastic in place.

9 Take one of the sleeve sections and fold it in half. Trace and transfer the Top Tees Pocket template to thin paper and cut it out to make your own template. Place the template on the sleeve, lining up the top edge of the template with the hemmed lower edge of the sleeve, then cut out the pocket. Press under and machine stitch 5mm (¼in) turnings around the sides and lower edge of the pocket.

10 Trace and transfer the Top Tees Flower and Leaf templates to thin card and cut them out to make your own templates. Draw around them onto scraps of contrasting T-shirt fabric and cut them out. Machine stitch them to the front of the pocket. Sew a contrasting button to the centre of the pocket. Pin the pocket to the front of the halter top, about 7.5cm (3in) above the lower edge, and machine stitch in place.

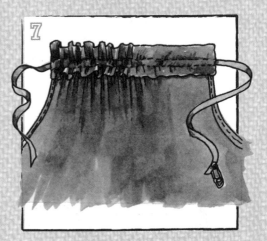

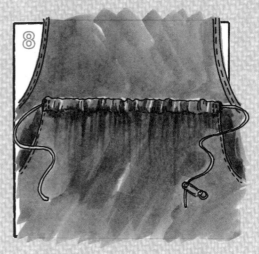

11 Follow Steps 1–8 to make the second halter top from the other XXL T-shirt.

12 Cut five 10cm (4in) circles from the off-cuts from the two T-shirts, two in one colour and three in the other. Fold four of the circles into quarters, and pin them to the centre of the fifth flat circle, alternating the colours. Stitch together with a few small stitches.

If you're feeling creative, simply grab and tie the excess fabric into a series of knots for a speedy tee-shirt makeover. There are some fab examples on the internet, so check out sewing and upcycling websites for inspiration.

13 Fan out the circles of fabric to make a rosette effect. Sew a button in the centre, then sew the rosette in position on the second halter top.

Get more...

» Don't dismiss **patterned T-shirts** that are very tired or worn. Take a close look and you may find **motifs** that you really love and that would look good cut out and **appliquéd** onto your halter top. Additionally, save any scraps of **cotton jersey** in **nice colours** and **patterns**, so that you have lots of options to choose from for adding **embellishments** to your tee tops.

» Try out your makeover ideas on old tees you don't want any more first of all. This way you can test run all your creative schemes and see whether they work, without ruining your favourite T-shirt. Also, you'd be amazed at how many fab effects you can achieve once you start playing around with T-shirts, so be brave and experiment before you commit yourself.

Although biggies are best, a skinny tee would also look good converted into a halter top.

» For a really simple T-shirt makeover:

1 **Remove** the **sleeves.**

2 **Snip open** the **seamlines** at the **tops** of the **armholes.**

3 **Tie** them back **together again**, gathering up the excess fabric tightly to make a really **snug fit.**

4 Get a friend to **pull in** the **excess fabric** at the **sides** and secure with **large safety pins** or **kilt pins**. If they show, then so much the better!

» I don't usually bother with finishing the raw edges of T-shirt fabric, as I don't find they fray. But if you want to **neaten seams**, **overstitch** the edges with a **very narrow zigzag** machine stitch. You can also use this to very good effect as a **decorative feature**, as it makes the fabric curl up slightly, creating an **attractive wavy edge.**

» Tees come in all sorts of fantastic colours and patterns (see photo right), so don't be shy about combining the wildest designs you can find!

Makeover
MAGIC

Whether you're trawling through tired old cardies in your bedroom or flicking through the racks in your favourite charity shop, once you've caught the upcycling bug, garments that you would have rejected without a second glance will seem ripe with possibility. You'll find yourself coveting unwearable tweed tailored jackets just because you like the colour or quality of the cloth. And vintage cotton pinnies will delight your eyes as you size them up for their unique potential.

Makeovers are all about being as creative as possible, so don't be tempted to stop just because you've adjusted something to fit better. The real joy is in the surprise elements – mixing materials, patterns and trims and adding ruffles, pleats and buttonholes makes all the difference.

Keep calm

I'm all for trying anything once, but I think it makes sense to keep a cool head when you've got makeover mania. Think carefully about what you want to achieve, before you reach for your purse or the sewing scissors. Although your basic ingredients will cost you little or nothing in terms of money, they are precious, because once you've cut them up there is no going back. Your time is also precious, and it's only worth investing time and effort in a project if you've got the right garments to start with, and you've done some constructive forward thinking.

Get inspired

I find flicking through fashion magazines hugely inspiring when I'm in the mood for a makeover. Here, I can find the latest info on length, colour and shape before I start cutting. It also helps me to decide what to choose for my latest project. You'll get plenty of new ideas by whizzing through a few upcycling websites too – there are loads around on the internet, and some are just so inspirational.

Choose wisely...

Try to avoid turning your house into one vast jumble sale! You'll need to think carefully about what will work when you're choosing clothes for a makeover. It's important to establish what your basic aims are, before you start, and to decide how much work you're prepared to do on your chosen garment. Think about the aspect of upcycling that most appeals to you. Are you an **updater** looking to breathe new life into an existing garment with a few clever tricks and a trim or two? Or are you more of a **deconstructer** willing to invest the time it takes to shake up and remake wardrobe basics by clever recutting and stitching?

If you're an **updater**, see the Cool Customizing feature for some quick and inventive embellishment ideas. Alternatively, if you're a **deconstructer**, see the Fabulous Fitting feature for tips on more major restructuring.

Rules of engagement

There are a few useful things to bear in mind when choosing your makeover garments. As long as you follow these rules, you won't go far wrong:

1 First and foremost, you're looking for attractive fabric. If you don't like the colour of last season's huge, baggy shirt, you won't find it any more appealing just because it fits better and you've added a few rows of sequins.

2 The second thing to look out for is quality. Don't pick anything that's gone bobbly in the wash, or has stretched out of all recognition. I like clothes made from cotton, linen, wool, corduroy and other natural fabrics because they're hardwearing, they fade nicely and they look great even when they're really well worn. They also keep their shape much better than manmade fabrics and are more pleasant to work with.

3 Finally, consider the weight of your garment. Is it too heavy to work with comfortably? Thick tweeds, denims and corduroy can be very frustrating and tiring to sew, and may not even fit under the foot of your sewing machine.

If you really get into restyling and recutting, you may find a tailoring course worthwhile, where you can learn lots of useful tips and tricks of the trade.

Tailor-made

Have a good look at any tailored jackets or coats that you find at the back of the wardrobe. They are perfect candidates for a bit of creative upcycling, especially if you originally paid a lot for them (see the Tailor Fit project). They're often made of good-quality cloth and lined with decent fabric, so they're definitely worth investing the time and effort of a serious makeover. If they're on the large side, they might only need a nip and tuck for the perfect fit. If you're feeling more ambitious, a complete makeover, with a new neckline, shorter sleeves or a radically altered silhouette, may tick the box. If they're just plain dull, consider new buttons, a flashy lining, funky trims or some quirky appliqué for an instant facelift.

Time travel

Keep an eye open for retro and retro-style household linens. Items such as curtains, tablecloths, embroidered napkins, patterned pillowcases, sheets and duvet (comforter) covers and vintage tea (dish) towels have great potential for trims and contrasting panels.

For smart ways to swap or sell your unwanted clothes and accessories, have a look at the Sewing Lounges and Swishing feature.

Sort it out

Once you've got a clear idea of the possibilities, and the amount of time you're willing to spend on each project, divide your clothes into groups:

• Make a pile of the things that only need a quick fix.

• Create another pile of clothes that would suit a more extensive makeover.

• It's worth keeping a box of items that are too far gone to wear but will yield scraps of fabric for trims and appliqué.

• The final group can be things like lovely scarves, bags, ties and belts that you can use to accessorize your makeovers.

Once you've sorted, it's time to organize a swap night or a trip to the charity shop for the remainder, because someone else will snap up anything you don't want!

Perfect PREPPING

Whenever I visit a charity shop or car boot/yard or nearly-new sale, I first let my eyes wander across the racks of old, unwanted clothes to see if any fabrics catch my eye. They nearly always do, and as I take promising garments off the rails for closer scrutiny, I hope they're good enough to upcycle into something new or with enough fabric to salvage and make into something special.

I then look for sad old woollies, shirts, dresses and skirts with great buttons or useful fastenings that can be harvested for a fraction of the cost of new items. My final trawl is for anything that can be taken apart and used as a pattern for a new version in my choice of fabric.

Stitch in time

If you like something enough to upcycle it with a snazzy makeover, take a hard look at it first to see if there are any major repairs you need to make:

- **Blouses** These are often a bit thin under the arms where the fabric has pulled and rubbed, so you may need to patch the wrong side of the material to repair a hole or a worn seam.

Try to make your patches as subtle as possible. You may find you can remove a section of fabric from an inconspicuous part of the garment to make a perfectly matched patch.

- **Trousers** These wear at the seat and knees, and seams ladder along stitches, especially if the fabric is manmade.

- **Seams** If the fabric has pulled away from a seam, you'll need to patch it, then cut away the old shredded areas before you start working that makeover magic.

Once holes are repaired, launder your garment, following the washing instructions, and you're ready to go.

Harvest time

If your fabulous find is too far gone to be upcycled, it's time to harvest what you can. To do this:

1 First wash and iron your garment.

2 Unpick and remove any lining.

3 Unpick all the seams, including any hems, darts, gathers or tucks.

4 Press the fabric flat.

5 The idea is to save as much usable fabric as possible, so check it over carefully for areas that are worn or rotten. If you're not sure, try gently tearing an inconspicuous section of the fabric. If it rips easily, it's probably rotten and unsuitable for reuse, so snip it out of the main fabric. You may find that the whole garment is in this state, in which case the best you can do, is to trim a section into a square and keep it for inspiration if you particularly like it.

6 Once you've saved everything you can, remove any buttons, zips and fastenings, and unpick trims like bias binding or ribbon.

7 Press the fabric again and trim off any uneven edges.

8 Wrap the fabric in tissue paper and keep it in a container until you need it for smaller projects like corsages, purses, bags, patchwork and cushion covers.

Perfect patterns

Keep a lookout for pattern potential in the form of items in really great classic shapes, for example A-line shift dresses, 50s sun dresses or little skirts, or maybe something by your favourite manufacturer – and the cheaper, the better.

Sometimes you'll find the garment of your dreams in fabric that you just can't stand, so snap it up, as long as it's the right price, create a pattern from it and remake it in a fabric of your choice!

To make your pattern:

1 Carefully unpick the garment (including hems, darts and gathers) and press all the pieces flat.

2 Draw around the fabric pieces onto thick paper, then cut the paper pieces out to make a pattern that you can reuse. Remember, you only need one for things like sleeves, as you'll cut them from a double thickness of fabric.

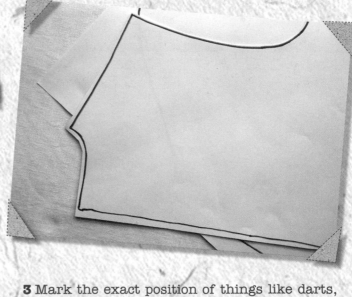

3 Mark the exact position of things like darts, pockets and zip openings onto the patterns so that you can transfer them to the fabric with tailor's tacks, tailor's chalk or transfer paper.

4 If the garment should have any interfacing, remember that you will need to make a pattern for this too.

Dig deep

Don't confine your search to clothes; some of my most exciting textiles are salvaged from household goods like sheets, pillowcases, duvet (comforter) covers, tea (dish) towels, towels, curtains and tablecloths. Bedding and tablecloths are a particularly good source of vividly patterned fabrics, especially if you're lucky enough to find originals from the 60s and 70s. Also, you get an awful lot of fabric for your money, so it's really worth checking out sales in department stores for bargain-priced sheets and duvet (comforter) covers, as well as scouring charity shops/thrift stores for second-hand versions.

Once you've tracked down a few treasures, cut away or repair any worn areas first before washing, unpicking and pressing.

Divide and rule

Before you put your salvaged fabrics away, it's worth sorting them into groups according to washing temperatures. Unless you're prepared to dry clean your upcycled creations (which isn't very green), remember not to mix different types of fabric in the same garment. Chances are, they won't all wash at the same temperature. If you group them before storing, it will make choosing fabrics for a new project a lot quicker and easier, and save much heartache in the long run. To be on the safe side, check out the washing instructions before you buy, and steer clear of anything that's dry clean only.

If there's no label and you're not sure of the fibre content of your salvaged fabrics, hand wash them and anything you make out of them in cool water only, to prevent disasters.

Storage savvy

Storing fabrics is a bit of an art form if you want to avoid digging through stacks of stuff when you need a particular colour or weight, so here's some handy advice:

• With old clothes, first salvage what you can in the way of zips and buttons, then wash, unpick and iron them.
• Fabric lengths should be pressed and folded into manageable sizes.
• I divide my clothes primarily by colour and keep them in a lidded crate.
• I store small fabric scraps in a box inside the crate so that they don't get lost in the general scrum.
• I tend to keep wools, denims and other heavy fabrics separate from lightweight cottons, so that I know at a glance what goes with what.

GET THE MOST FROM...

Your ACCESSORIES

Best-Dress(ed) Bag

This gorgeous bag is refashioned from an adorable little velvet dress that sadly no longer fitted my daughter. I haven't altered the basic shape and style of the dress, just chopped off the skirt section and made a gusset at the base of the bag for extra room. A professional look is achieved by adding a pair of fab leather handles, salvaged from an otherwise unlovely handbag.

Get into it...

Dress it up

Little girls' dresses make lovely handbags; they're just the right size to carry all your essentials, and they're the perfect shape for attaching new handles. I've used a sleeveless pinafore dress for this project, but if you find a long-sleeved dress you love, simply unpick and remove the sleeves, then hem the raw edges around the armholes before you begin sewing.

Tough it out

Bags take an awful lot of day-to-day wear and tear, so choose a dress in good-quality fabric for your bag, and if it's lined, so much the better. Heavyweight, natural materials like cotton velvet, corduroy and denim are ideal fabrics to go for, because they're hardwearing and easy to sew. They'll also age gracefully, and slide gently into a shabby-chic old age.

Handle with care

You can get pairs of handles from craft suppliers and bag manufacturers online, but they're often pricey, especially when you can pick up tatty second-hand or downright nasty bags for next to nothing yet with attractive handles that are very easy to remove. Look for handles with pre-punched holes so that you can simply unpick them and re-attach them to your bag. I find it's best to use waxed thread to stitch them on. This is very strong, thick thread that is waxed to help it glide through sturdy materials like leather.

Make the most of it

Try to incorporate features like buttons and zips into your bag design, as it's much easier than trying to remove or conceal them. For example, in this project I used a dress with a back zip. I knew I couldn't hide the zip without removing it altogether, so I incorporated it into my design by making it the bag opening. You could do the same by leaving the pocket on the front of a pinafore dress (useful for notebooks), or sewing a handy key ring into side pockets.

Get it together...

* Child's dress and matching thread
* Ruler and fine marker pen
* Scissors
* Pins
* Sewing machine
* Iron
* Hand sewing needle
* Salvaged bag handles
* Reusable putty adhesive (optional)
* Scraps of pink and green felted wool
* Shirring elastic
* Tracing paper and thin card
* Safety pin or brooch back

1 Measure from the top of the dress to the length that you want your bag to be. Draw a straight line from one side of the dress to the other at this point, then trim the dress to size, through both layers of fabric.

2 Turn the dress inside out and turn back the lining. Draw a line 1.5cm (⅝in) above the lower edge of the dress. Pin the layers of the dress together, then machine stitch along the line. Overstitch the raw edges of the fabric below the seam line.

3 To make a flat base at the bottom of the bag, press open the side and base seams. Press each corner flat so that the base and side seams are aligned and measure in 3cm (1¼in) at either side. Draw a guideline across each corner of the bag, and machine stitch. Trim away the excess fabric. Do the same with the bag lining.

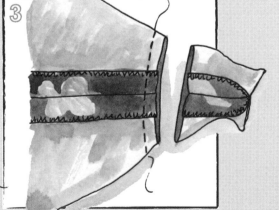

4 At the top of the bag, snip across the seams at the shoulders to separate them. Press under the dress fabric and lining by 5mm (¼in) to conceal the raw edges. Slip stitch the edges together. Unpick the handles from your original bag and position the ends at the top of the shoulders on the front and back of the bag. Hold them in place with a little reusable putty adhesive if you wish, then hand sew them in position, using the original stitch holes.

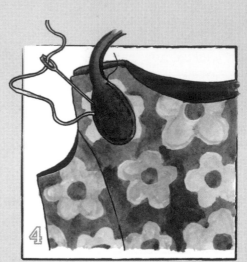

5 To make the rose corsage, cut a 40cm (16in) long x 4cm (1½in) wide strip of pink felted wool. Wind shirring elastic onto an empty bobbin and place it in your sewing machine. Using a fairly long stitch, sew along one edge of the strip to gather it gently. Cut a wavy edge along the ungathered side of the strip. Tightly roll up the gathered edge to make a rose shape. Turn the rose over and slip stitch the edges to keep them together.

6 Trace and transfer the Best-Dress(ed) Bag Leaf template to thin paper and cut it out to make your own template. Use to cut three leaves from felted green wool, then sew to the back of the rose. Slip stitch a safety pin or brooch back to the centre back of the rose and pin it to the bag.

Get more...

» Can't find handles you like? Simply make a pair from two long strips of fabric in a contrasting colour, or recycle an old belt. If you want really cool handles, try:

• using **two completely different** belts

• using one in really **wild colours**, **patterns** or **textures**, such as **mock croc** or **snakeskin**, **glitter** or **sequins**

» Why not make yourself a corsage to wear too? An oversize one in contrasting or matching felted scraps would look great on a jacket or cardi for a cool, coordinated look. These corsages also make great little Christmas stocking fillers and birthday presents by themselves, and you can whip up a few in an evening.

Look out for retro wooden knitting bag handles and solid wood or plastic circular styles, which are all ultra stylish.

» Want a bag for a friend's wedding or a teenager's prom? Scour your daughters' and nieces' wardrobes (or your nearest charity shop, if they look less than impressed) for **dresses** and **blouses** they've grown out of. These unwanted gems will make fab little **evening** or **special occasion bags**, especially in delicate **silky**, **satiny synthetic fabrics**. To cheer them up once you've plundered their wardrobes, make them a bag too, and they'll love you forever!

If you want to know more about social sewing, check out the Sewing Lounges and Swishing feature.

» A really big occasion coming up that you're all going to? Why not organize a swaporama-and-sew evening for friends. Get them to bring their unwanted goodies over so that you can all rummage around and bag something you like. Then gossip, laugh and enjoy the refreshments while you await your turn at the sewing machine.

» Going out in an hour and no time to make a corsage? Grab a **sparkly brooch** and **pin** it in its place on the **bag** – it will also look great and has the added bonus of being removable, so your bag will look different every time that you use it.

Arm Artwork

I love arm-warmers – they're warm and cosy, and the perfect way to add a bit of oomph to an outfit without breaking the bank. You can glam them up for a special occasion, and they're practical enough for everyday wear too. They couldn't be easier to make either; all you need are a few off-cuts from your favourite old woollies and away you go.

Get into it...

Put on the glitz

I decided to make a very girly pair of arm-warmers using lovely sugary colours and pretty contrasts, and spent quite a lot of time playing around with colour combinations before deciding on the final bits and pieces I wanted to use. I chose the sequinned waistband of an old evening cardi to make the trim at the tops of the sleeves because I thought it looked so glam.

Select sleeves

You can use whatever bits of your old woolly you like to make arm-warmers, but sleeves are the best starting point because they are shaped, and usually have a ribbed cuff section. This will fit very nicely over your own wrist, pulling the fabric in neatly and holding it gently in place. Choose a woolly that fits you well.

Fab felting

You don't have to stick to pure wool for your arm-warmers, but it gives you the option of felting your stash of chosen woollies before you begin. Felted woollies are thick and warm, water-repellent and don't fray, so can save you time in not having to finish the edges. Pure (100%) wool, synthetic yarn or a wool/synthetic mix are all good for arm-warmers, but remember not to mix them unless you've felted or pre-shrunk everything together at the same temperature.

Sequins are a great addition to arm-warmers, so if you can't find a sparkly sweater to plunder, sew on a few as a finishing touch.

For instructions on how to felt woollies, see the Nifty Knits feature.

The finishing touch

If you've used unfelted woollies, don't forget to finish off your edges. Your arm-warmers will fray if you don't, especially when you wash them. It's easy to make sure they stay in one piece – simply sew a row of very small zigzag stitches over the raw edges of each seam to keep all the threads together.

* Felted woolly sweater or cardigan and
  felted wool scraps and matching
  thread
* Ruler and marker pen
* Scissors
* Pins
* Sewing machine
* Iron
* Small coin
* Shirring elastic
* Hand sewing needle
* Tracing paper and pencil
* Thin card
* 2 buttons for the corsage
  and matching thread

1 Cut two sections 20cm (8in) long from the arms of the woolly sweater or cardigan, keeping the ribbed wrist sections in place. Cut two 8cm (3¼in) bands from contrasting sleeves to trim the tops of the arm-warmers.

2 Cut open all the sleeve sections along the seams. Pin the trim sections on top of the arm sections along the unribbed sides. Machine stitch the trims to the arms.

3 To make the sections that cover the hands, cut two pieces 12cm (4¾in) long of contrasting sleeve section and cut open along the seams. Pin and machine stitch to the arm sections, with wrong sides facing.

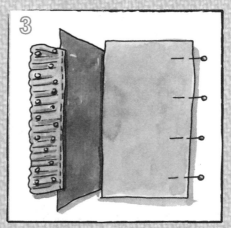

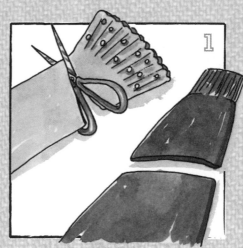

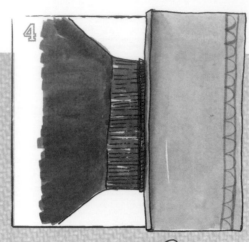

4 Press open the seams on the backs of the arm-warmers. Rule straight lines along the tops of the hand sections, about 3cm (1¼in) down from the top edge. Place a small coin along the lines and draw around the top half to make a row of semicircles. Cut out to make a scalloped edge.

5 Fold the arm-warmers lengthways in half, right sides together, and pin the long seams. Machine stitch the sides together, then trim away the excess fabric. Try on the arm-warmers and snip a small hole for each thumb.

6 To make the ruffle trims, cut a long strip of contrasting woolly, about 3cm (1¼in) wide. Wind shirring elastic onto an empty bobbin and place it in your sewing machine. Using matching thread and a fairly long stitch, sew down the centre of the strip to ruffle it and then cut a length to fit around the top of each arm-warmer. Pin over the seams of the trims, then slip stitch in place.

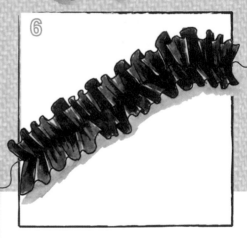

To make the corsage

Trace and transfer the Arm Artwork Flower and Leaf templates to thin card and cut out. Draw around the templates onto your felted wool scraps and cut out. Hand sew the leaves to the back of the flower, then sew the corsage in place on one arm-warmer, stitching through a large and medium button, one on top of the other, in the centre.

Get more...

» Look over your woollies with a critical eye before you start to make your arm-warmers. Are there any sections you could salvage that would make a **ready-made trim**, or an **eye-catching middle section**? Even the holiest old sleeves usually have some redeeming features!

Woolly tights also make ideal arm-warmers, as they fit really closely and don't need seaming.

» If you're over arm-warmers, why not make a pair of **fingerless gloves** instead? They look great, and they're just like arm-warmers but without the long upper section. Try to salvage the **ribbed wrist sections** from your old woollies to make your gloves, as they will improve the fit no end.

» Decorating your arm-warmers with a motif makes them really special:

• You can cut out **all kinds of shapes** from leftover **felted wool scraps** (as with the corsage) so that the edges won't fray and add details with **sequins, beads** or **buttons**.

• If you're feeling adventurous, **machine appliqué** onto your arm-warmers before you seam them; use a **contrasting thread** and stitch quite messily around your motifs for a **fun** and **funky** look (see photo below).

» Take a little time to play around with your sections of woolly before you decide on a scheme for your arm-warmers. Be brave and try out **bold contrasts** of colour and texture for the most interesting designs (see photo above). Have a good root round your local charity shop for woollies made from **angora** or **mohair**. Not only will they be amazingly soft to the touch and a delight to wear, even small sections would make a great focal point around the tops or fingers.

» For the **60-second version** of the arm-warmer, simply chop an arm-length section from an old sleeve and snip a hole for your thumb. This gives you a fantastic blank canvas to add little designer details such as a few sequins or a couple of buttons and a bow. However yours turn out, you can be sure that no one else will have a pair quite the same!

For an alternative chic design for a pair of motif-decorated arm-warmers, check out the Mono Hat-Trick project.

Character Charms

What do you get when you start upcycling the contents of your wardrobe? A load of fab leftovers such as fabric off-cuts, buttons, zips and fastenings. And what should you do with them? Make them into charms and plushies of course! Children love decorating their school bags with charms, and they're so quick, fun and easy to make, they're the perfect project to enjoy with kids.

Get into it...

Roll up

Try to think creatively when you're making charms from leftovers. Often a button or a pattern on a piece of fabric will remind me of something else. For example, I'd accumulated a pile of zips and didn't know what to make with them. First of all I tried to curve them into flower corsages, but couldn't get the petals even, so then I rolled up the zips to make flower centres. This idea worked, but the zips also reminded me of eyes and hair, so I ended up making the zippy plushie instead.

Button it

If, like me, you've got loads of spare buttons, you can make the most fantastically decorative charms with them. There's something really satisfying about a sparkly, button-encrusted surface, and the more mismatched the buttons, the better. I decided on a heart-shaped charm, so cut two from a double layer of felted woolly sweater. I went for brightly coloured buttons to decorate the hearts, adding a large button at the centre to make a focal point. I thought the edges looked a bit unfinished, so I dug out a stash of heart-shaped buttons left over from a workshop, and sewed them around the charm to make a pretty edging.

Get rough and tough

Go to any high-street fashion store and you'll find loads of different charms in every shape, colour and size. I was inspired to make the monkey by a denim teddy bear charm I spotted in a department store. I love denim anyway, but it particularly appealed to me for charm making because it's tough and hardwearing, and easy and cheap to find in charity shops and car boot/yard sales. I like the fact that denim frays, and the edges of the charm will gradually become more ragged and characterful.

Sock it to 'em

The zippy plushie is made from the toe section of an old pair of school tights (pantyhose). I chose the dark colour because it sets off the brightly coloured zips so nicely. Tights and socks are perfect for making charms and plushies, especially if they're very colourful or highly patterned. Tiny baby socks make really dinky little charms, while there's enough fabric in most adult socks to make plushie dolls and animals.

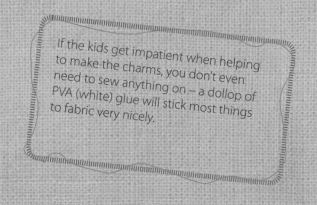

If the kids get impatient when helping to make the charms, you don't even need to sew anything on – a dollop of PVA (white) glue will stick most things to fabric very nicely.

Flower Power

* Scrap of floral fabric and matching or contrasting thread
* Scissors
* Pins
* Sewing machine
* Contrasting button
* Ribbon and matching thread
* Split ring
* Hand sewing needle

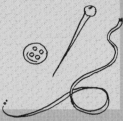

1 Choose a flower motif from your fabric scrap and roughly cut it out. Pin it to a second layer of fabric and machine stitch around the outline several times, then cut it out. Sew a contrasting-coloured button to the centre of the flower.

2 Cut a 30cm (12in) length of ribbon and thread it through a split ring. Machine stitch the sides of the ribbon together, stopping about 3cm (1¼in) from the split ring. Hand stitch the ribbon ends to the back of the flower.

Zippy Plushie

1. Cut 20cm (8in) from the top of the foot of the pair of woolly tights (pantyhose). Cut the end off a red zip and pull it apart to give two halves. Cut a 25cm (10in) section of the zip and curve it round to make the mouth. Roll up a 2cm-(¾in-) deep fold in the tights about halfway down the foot. Roll down a second fold just above the first. Insert the zip into the folds to make the mouth and hand stitch in place.

2. Lightly stuff the foot of the tights and slip stitch the opening closed to make the head. To make the hair, separate a yellow zip, roll up the ends to make curls and pin in place. Slip stitch the edges of the curls together. Sew the hair to the top of the head. Roll up the eyes from yellow and blue zips, and stitch them in place. Sew a button below the eyes for the nose.

3. Cut an oval from your scrap of red felted wool and glue inside the mouth. Cut a short section of zip and fold it into a bow. Stitch it to the top of the head, then stitch a button on top. Sew a length of contrasting-coloured zip around the neck of the plushie.

Get it together...

* Pair of dark blue woolly tights (pantyhose) and matching thread
* Scissors
* Coloured zips including red, yellow and blue
* Hand sewing needle
* Stuffing (cut-up nylon tights are really good)
* Pins
* 2 buttons
* Scrap of red felted wool
* PVA (white) glue

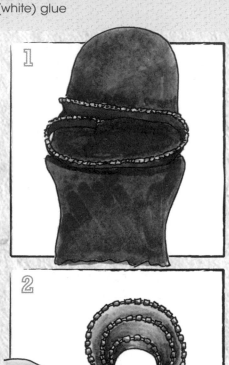

Monkey Mate

1 Trace and transfer the Monkey Mate template to thin card and cut out to make your own template. Draw around the template onto an off-cut of denim and cut it out. Pin it to a larger off-cut of denim. Slip two folded pieces of ribbon between the layers at either side of the monkey's head to make ears. Add a loop of ribbon at the top. Machine stitch around the edge of the monkey with contrasting thread. Leave a gap so that you can stuff the monkey.

2 Stuff the monkey, then machine stitch the opening closed. Sew buttons on for the eyes and glue a piece of red ric rac below the eyes to make the mouth. Tie a piece of ribbon around the monkey's neck to make a scarf. Add a split ring and clip to the ribbon loop at the top of the monkey.

Get it together...

* Off-cuts of denim and contrasting thread
* Tracing paper and pencil
* Thin card
* Scissors
* Pins
* Narrow ribbon in 3 different colours/ designs
* Sewing machine
* Stuffing
* Buttons
* Hand sewing needle
* Red ric rac
* PVA (white) glue
* Split ring and clip

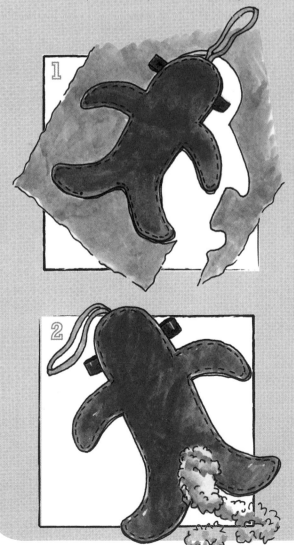

Button Love

Get it together...

* Scrap of felted wool
* Paper
* Scissors
* Pen
* Pins
* Selection of coloured buttons, including small shaped buttons for edging
* Hand sewing needle and thread
* Narrow ribbon
* Split ring and clip

1 To make the template, fold a piece of paper in half and cut one side of a heart shape. Draw around the template onto a double thickness of felted wool in any colour. Pin the two layers together, then cut them out.

2 Hand sew a random pattern of buttons to the heart, and finish the centre with a larger button. Sew small shaped buttons around the edge of the heart to make a decorative edging.

3 Cut a 30cm (12in) length of narrow ribbon and thread it through the split ring attached to the metal clip, doubling the tape to make a loop. Sew the tape to the back of the charm to keep it in place.

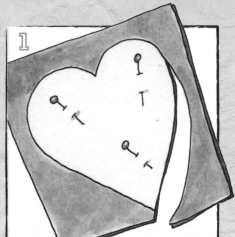

Get more...

» I've noticed that initials and words are really popular charms, especially with children. A quick and fun idea for a child's birthday present is to cut their **initials** or a **single word** from **felted wool**, then lightly stuff it and decorate it with **sequins**, **sparkly buttons** or whatever else appeals.

» I love the interesting colour variations in **faded denim**, and the dark patches left when you remove pockets and belts loops. Try to incorporate these **light** and **dark areas** when you're making your charms. For example, if you carefully unpick the **pockets** from the back of a pair of **jeans**, you'll find interesting **dark areas** that could become a charm **character's hair**, or represent its **trousers**. Place your pattern carefully on the denim to make the most of colour variations before you cut out your fabric.

Charms make fun accessories for handbags too, so have a look through your stash and see what inspires you.

» **Plushies** are soft, squashy cuddly toys, usually of **cartoon characters**, and have become a **mega craze**. Go online to check out the subject and you'll be amazed at what you'll find. They are especially popular in Japan, and there many websites, blogs and books devoted to the subject. My favourites are the little animal characters known collectively as '*kawaii*' in Japanese, which means cute or sweet, but there's an amazing array of designs out there to inspire you.

» Felted woolly sweaters are perfect for making charms and plushies, but if you don't have any leftovers, don't despair. **Socks** and **woolly tights (pantyhose)**, **fleecy fabric**, **corduroy** and **denim** are great too, and the more **battered** and **characterful** the fabric, the better. Don't forget to harvest **buttons**, **zips**, **fasteners**, **sections of buttonhole** and so on from every single garment you recycle – they will make **fantastic facial** features for all your charms and plushies.

On a budget? Keep your eyes open in charity shops/thrift stores for jars of mismatched buttons to use for making your charms.

Mono Hat-Trick

I adored this hat the moment I set eyes on it. I immediately thought Audrey Hepburn and those stunning black and white Cecil Beaton costumes she wore at the races in the movie *My Fair Lady*, so I decided to give it a monochrome makeover. In my rummage for felted wool for the floral detail, I found a black cashmere sweater that had shrunk in the wash, which I recycled into coordinating arm-warmers and a corsage.

Get into it...

Get ahead

Look for a hat with an interesting shape that suggests a stylistic theme to you. A sharp trilby or a soft floppy hat can be treated in very different ways, and often a look will pop into your head as soon as you find the right hat. My chosen hat evoked the 60s and Audrey Hepburn, and in turn the black and white scheme, which has been used to great effect by some of the most influential fashion designers. When op art was all the rage, designers such as Mary Quant (creator of the mini skirt) introduced a cool, pared-down style with a much simpler, bolder use of colour contrasts. Black and white was also an intrinsic part of the Mod look of the 60s. I started by removing the original green stripy ribbon from the hat to restore the basic shape.

A stitch in time

I wanted a cool retro makeover to echo the 60s feel of the hat. I also wanted a smart, tailored look, as I felt this would work very well with the monochrome colour scheme. I liked the idea of a ribbon band, but decided on a narrow, elegant stripe as a subtle counterpoint to a bold and eye-catching floral embellishment. To tie in with the dapper, tailored effect, I chose a hand-stitched border around the rim of the hat. This gave the hat an upmarket feel, reminiscent of tailored suits, so the hat would look good with more formal clothing. I also added a row of contrasting stitches along the centre of the ribbon band before I attached it, echoing the tailored theme.

Turn to the Nifty Knits feature for complete instructions on how to felt your woollens.

Well armed

To continue the timeless, more formal look, I decided to make a pair of complementary arm-warmers. I had a beautiful, extremely soft cashmere sweater that had been accidentally felted by a friend of mine in a hot machine wash. Bad news for her, but it cheered her up to think that that her woolly was being upcycled into these cool gloves-with-a-difference, complete with accent trim, and a tassel corsage to match.

Woolly thinking

The basis for all three accessories is felted wool. Once more, this project illustrates just how useful it is as a source of easily obtainable fabric in a wide range of colours. The best thing about felted wool is that once the fibres have been processed in hot water, they just won't fray, so don't need any complicated finishing or hemming. This leaves you free to experiment with all the different effects you can create simply by rolling and cutting.

* Hat and contrasting thread
* Scraps of felted wool in 2 contrasting light and dark colours, felted woollen cardigan or sweater and contrasting and matching thread
* Ruler and thin marker pen
* Scissors
* Hand sewing needle
* 3 sets of 2 contrasting buttons
* Tracing paper and pencil
* Thin card
* Fabric glue
* Narrow contrasting ribbon and contrasting thread
* Safety pin

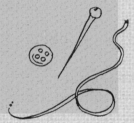

1. To make the flower for the hat, cut two contrasting pieces of felted wool measuring 4cm x 14cm (1½in x 5½in). Make cuts along one long side of each piece, stopping about 1cm (⅜in) below the top edge, to create a fringed effect.

2. Place the pieces of wool one on top of the other, carefully lining up the top edges. Roll them together to make a tassel. Sew a few stitches through the base of the tassel to keep it securely rolled. Turn over the tassel and fan out the snipped edges to form the flower. In the middle of the flower, flatten the petals and sew two contrasting buttons, one on top of the other, to make the centre.

3. Trace and transfer the Mono Hat-Trick Leaf and Vein templates to thin card and cut out to make your own templates. Use to cut six leaf shapes from the light-coloured felted wool and three veins from the dark. Sew or glue the light leaves together in pairs, then glue the veins onto each pair. Glue the flower head and petals to the side of the hat with fabric glue.

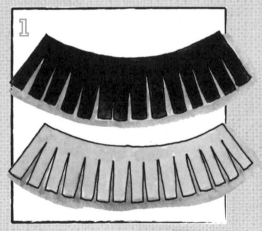

4　Cut a length of ribbon to fit around the crown of the hat, with a 2cm (¾in) overlap. Sew a line of contrasting running stitches along the length of the ribbon. Attach the ribbon around the crown of the hat with fabric glue. Sew a line of contrasting running stitches around the rim of the hat.

5　For the arm-warmers, cut the sleeves off a felted woollen garment. Sew a line of contrasting running stitches around the cuffs. Cut long, 1cm- (⅜in-) wide strips from a piece of contrasting felted wool. Form the strips of wool into loops. Stitch through the base of the loops and draw them together in a circle to form a flower shape. Sew a flower to the front of each arm-warmer, above the cuffs. Sew two contrasting buttons to the centres of the flowers.

6　For the corsage, cut two contrasting pieces of felted wool measuring 4cm x 20cm (1½in x 8in). Make cuts along one long side of each piece, as for the hat flower. Roll the two pieces of wool together to make a tassel. Sew a few stitches through the base to keep it in place. Sew a safety pin to the back.

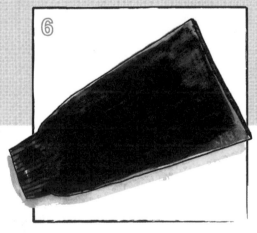

Get more...

» **Is the flower a bit over the top for you?** Simply adding a **contrasting ribbon** around the **crown** of the hat can make a stylish impact. Fancy ribbon can be very expensive, so it makes sense to recycle a length you've removed from another garment if at all possible. **Plain satin** or **velvet ribbon** are ideal options for hatbands.

» **Leather** or **fabric belts** make **great hatbands** (see photo right). Fabric belts are especially good, as they're soft enough to manipulate around the crown of the hat. Leave the **buckle** in place as a cool feature! **Patterned ties** are also excellent candidates for hatbands (see photo below).

» As decorative ribbon can be so expensive, I like to **upcycle** my own **ribbon**, for example with **running stitch**, as in this project, or with a row of **sequins**, **gemstones** or **mother-of-pearl buttons**. For this, I always use **grosgrain** ribbon – a sturdy, lightly ribbed ribbon – as it won't pucker when stitched and it's thick enough to absorb fabric glue.

» If full-length arm-warmers aren't your thing, experiment with the length of the sleeves until you find what works the best. The felted wool won't fray, so you can cut it to any length and shape without fear of it unravelling. **Mitten** or **glove length** works just as well, and you get all the style benefits without any of the bulk.

» You can apply all sorts of decorative ideas to your arm-warmers:

• Try **snipping small holes** and **shapes** out of the arms for a **cobweb effect**.

• Add **stick-on gems** and **sequins** for a **glam sparkly look**.

• **Lines** of **running stitch** look great, as do simple **embroidered designs**.

• Look out for **attractive bits** that you can salvage from **old woollies** to **appliqué** around your arm-warmers (see photo right). This gives you a fantastic blank canvas for adding designer details such as a few sequins or a row of simple embroidery stitches.

Nifty KNITS

Woollen sweaters and cardigans make perfect subjects for upcycling. With just a few well-judged tweaks they can be transformed into glam garments, or felted in hot water and then reconstructed into something completely new. Once you've discovered the endless potential of old knits, you'll start reassessing your wardrobe with a keen eye to explore the possibilities.

Learn how to spot the potential in a battered old item and start pilfering stuff from your friends or rescuing wonderful woollies from charity shops and at car boot/yard sales. This is where going to swaporamas and swishing events will pay dividends – you may be the only person who sees the beauty in a tired old cardi, while others are fighting over the more popular garments.

Keen upcycler WLTM...

...the perfect woolly! Which is anything that has style potential. It might catch your eye because it's a lovely colour, has a funky pattern or is a nice shape. Even if stained or holey, smaller areas may be worth salvaging for a bag, purse, belt or mittens. Look for hues and patterns that you really like, especially if you're felting – no amount of clever cutting will disguise the fact that the woolly you started out with is an unappetizing beige. Also avoid anything knitted from scratchy wool, as it will irritate your skin even more once felted.

To felt or not to felt?

You don't need to felt your woollies before you reuse them. If you've discovered a well-fitting yet dull cardi or sweater in the most amazing shade, you can simply recut it and revamp it with a few trims for a fast, cool makeover. But if you've got a pile of tired old woollies that no amount of restyling will salvage, then it's worth felting them. Felting woollies (or 'fulling', as it is traditionally known) produces a dense, fuzzy material that won't fray when it's cut. Felted wool is warm and repels water, and is used in many cultures to make clothing, shoes and even dwellings (think Mongolian yurts). Even scraps are worth reusing in this way – the baggy old sleeves left over from upcycling a sweater can be felted, then chopped up and transformed into fab accessories such as corsages and arm-warmers.

Even odd scraps of nice knits are worth rescuing – bands can be stitched together to make a stripy scarf, thin strips gathered to create a ruffled edging (see the Cardi Creative project) or small bits used to make an appliqué detail on a tweedy garment or hat (see the Mono Hat-Trick project).

What to felt

- Sweaters and cardies composed of at least 90% wool or animal fibres
- Medium-weight machine-knitted woollies
- Hand-knitted, medium-stitch woollies

What not to felt

- Sweaters and cardies composed of less than 90% wool or animal fibres
- Fine knits – these will go limp in a hot wash
- Chunky kits – these make felt that's too dense to manipulate easily
- Shrink-proof woollies – these are treated with chemicals to prevent shrinking and will stubbornly refuse to get smaller; if you persevere, the most these knits will do is bleed their dye into the washing machine in large quantities!

It's OK if your woolly contains some nylon, but if the content is higher than 10%, it won't shrink satisfactorily.

Get felting

To successfully felt your woollies, follow these easy stages:

Stage one

Machine wash them with detergent on a hot cycle. The washing agitates the wool, matting the fibres together to leave a dense, felted surface. Felting woollies isn't an exact science and that's what makes it so exciting. You can never tell just how much they will shrink, or how well they will felt, so you may have to put your sweater through the wash more than once to achieve the desired effect.

Stage two

Once your woolly is washed, a whizz through a hot tumble dryer will fluff up the felted surface, matting it even more densely. The heat will also kill off any moth problems – especially useful if your woolly has been stored for a long time.

Stage three

Once your woolly is dry, check it to see if it's felted enough. If the wool resembles felt and doesn't fray when you cut into it, the process has been successful. If not, you'll need to repeat the washing and drying actions until it no longer frays. Don't cut your woollies up before you felt them – it's easier to keep them flat and straight while still in one piece.

Stage four

A good press with a steam iron will help to reshape and remove any stubborn creases before you begin work on your woolly. Felted wool often needs a bit of steam to finish the surface before cutting and sewing.

Top Felting Tips

- Put your woollies inside a pillowcase when machine washing, to stop the surface bobbling.
- Add them to the machine with a heavy load, such as towels, to increase the amount of friction and enhance the felting process.

It's a stitch-up

You can hand stitch or machine stitch woollen knits in exactly the same way as any other fabric. Machine stitching is a cinch if you use the right stitches and needles, and hand stitching is great for adding a fiddly bit of trim or a row of contrasting, decorative stitches.

When sewing knitted fabrics with a machine, pin the pieces together as normal, then swap your usual needle for a ballpoint needle. This has a rounded tip that threads through knitted fabric without cutting the fibres, as a sharp needle would do. It also prevents the needle point from making runs in finely knitted fabrics like stretch jerseys, so is great for sewing upcycled T-shirts. As with universal sewing machine needles, ballpoint needles come in different gauges suitable for different weights of fabric, from fine to heavy.

Use a **medium-length stitch** when sewing woollies and a **textured polyester** or **nylon thread**, which has more elasticity than cotton.

Keeping in shape

When you're simply restyling an unfelted woolly, you'll need to stay stitch and finish off the raw edges to prevent them from stretching and fraying. This is especially important if the garment is curved, as curves stretch more than straight edges.

Stay stitching This line of medium-length stitching is sewn through one layer of fabric 5mm (¼in) from the edge to stabilize it. It's particularly useful on knitted wool fabrics, which tend to stretch and distort very easily.

Overstitching To prevent fraying, finish off raw edges on unfelted wool with a line of overstitching, using the overlocking foot and stitching option on your machine. If your machine doesn't have one, machine stitch a line of small zigzag stitches over the cut edge to finish them off securely and neatly.

Fabulous
FITTING

It's all very well upcycling a boring old dress into a ravishing little cocktail number or cutting down an enormous jacket into a groovy gilet, but how do you get them to fit you properly? While it's easy enough to shorten legs and sleeves, what if the waist, chest or hips are far too big? The answer is to reshape the fabric so that it will flow over the curves of your body.

Fabric shaping is very simple once you know how. At its most basic level (unless you're into haute couture), it's about reducing the fullness with darts, or by using gentle pleats, tucks and gathers. Once you know the ins and outs of basic alteration, you'll also be able to tweak any new clothes for an improved fit.

Dart design

Darts are triangular seams that sculpt the fabric so that a straight piece of fabric can be curved over rounded areas like the arms, bust, shoulders and hips. They are traditionally placed where the figure is fullest, across the upper body and above and below the waistline. This helps to shape the garment, providing fullness where needed and decreasing areas that are too bulky in order that the fabric lies flat.

Sewing books are an enormous help in showing you where darts and tucks should be, although your garment may already have both.

For a better-fitting dress:
• Unpick and resew the original darts to make them wider and to take in more fabric.
• If there's a lot of excess fabric, sew in a couple of extra darts next to the originals, and add a couple of tucks if you need to. This distributes the fullness evenly and creates a smoother silhouette.

For a better-fitting skirt:
• First remove the waistband.
• Adjust the darts, then replace the waistband, shortening it if necessary.

Work it out

I often try on a dress or skirt only to find that the hips fit me nicely but the waist is too small. To make it fit, I could just take in the side seams, but this might decrease the fullness in the wrong area or pull the garment out of shape. Also, if the dress has a side zip, or the skirt has pockets, they'll get in the way and make any adjustments impossible. Therefore, a more subtle, targeted approach is called for. If you have a paper pattern that's similar to the garment you want to reshape, take a close look at it to see where the darts, tucks and gathers are positioned. You can often use a pattern in this way as a guide for your own makeover.

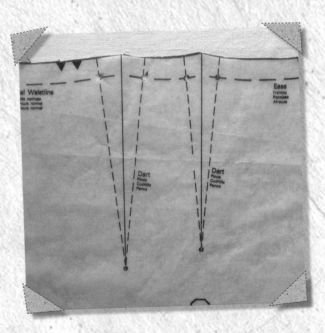

Size it up

Sometimes you'll be starting from scratch, with no original darts or tucks to guide you. Or you may be reshaping something bulky, like a lined jacket. If so, you'll need to make your own alterations, which will involve working out how much fabric to take in at either side. To do this:

1 Try on the garment and pin or clamp the excess fabric with mini bulldog clips on the right side of the clothing until it fits you snugly. This will tell you by how much you need to reduce the fullness.

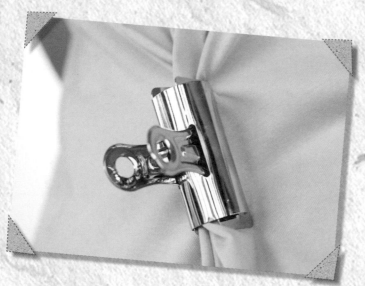

2 Remove the garment and then unpick the lining as far as you need to in order that you can reach the area you're working on from the inside.

3 Measure and check that you have pinned an equal amount of fabric on either side, then turn your garment inside out.

4 Remove the pins or clips, one at a time, and carefully transfer and pin the fullness to the wrong side of the fabric. Draw a stitching line down the length of the dart with tailor's chalk, then tack (baste) it in place.

5 Try on your garment again to check the fit, then machine stitch the dart.

If you've got a dressmaker's dummy, then this is the time to dust it down. It can be adjusted to match your own height and body measurements, and will make checking your alterations a lot easier (unless you've got a willing friend who is roughly the same proportions as you).

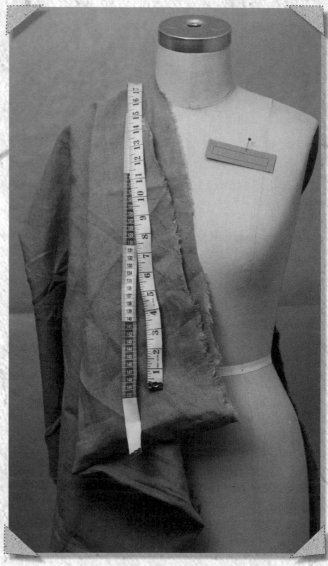

Turn it up

So you've adjusted your garment and now it fits you nicely, but what if the arms or legs are still too long? You could chop them to size and bind them with contrasting or similar fabric, as in the example pictured right, but for a simple shortening job, follow these three easy steps:

1 Turn your garment inside out and unpick any lining from around the original hems.

2 Turn up the excess fabric to the right length, then pin it and try the garment on for size. If it looks good, press the turning in place on the wrong side, trim off any excess fabric and press under the raw edges by about 1cm (⅜in).

3 Slip stitch the hems in place using matching thread. Trim and press under the lining in the same way and slip stitch back into place.

Make sure that you use a compatible fabric for your turn-ups so that your garment can be successfully laundered. Otherwise, be prepared to hand wash it, to err on the side of caution.

Dart and tuck know-how

• **Hip and waist darts** These are sewn vertically above and below the waistline.

• **Bust darts** These can run horizontally or on the diagonal. When you add in a bust dart, angle the point upwards so that it follows the line of the body more closely.

• **Matching darts** In the case of waist and hip darts, or tucks, you're aiming to distribute the fullness of the fabric evenly around the mid section, so each tuck and dart needs to take in an equal amount of fabric, or the garment will end up looking lopsided. So measure and mark carefully before you start sewing.

GET THE MOST FROM...

Your CARE & REPAIR

Jean Genius

I just love the way that denim jeans fade and wear. It's always a sad moment for me when a favourite pair gets a bit past it, so I store them up for ages while I work out the best way to salvage the fabric. Jeans are the one item of clothing that you can't go over the top with, so follow my example and add patches, fabric inserts and studs, or reach for the bleach!

Get into it...

Pick your pair with care

A pair of jeans with the odd rip and tear, or trodden-in hems, is just asking for a makeover. But one with no knees and a worn seat isn't really worth all the hard work of adding a bit of bling. Once the fabric has started to rot and wear thin, there's nothing you can do to save it, so the best solution is to cut away the bits that are still okay and save them for patching and appliqué work.

Ripping yarn

Jeans are made from tough fabric, held together with heavy stitching. The seams are quite tricky to unpick, as they're often double stitched. The only thing to do is use a quick-unpick, or seam ripper, and an awful lot of patience. Seam rippers are handy little gadgets with a sharp blade that rips quickly through rows of stitching. Take care not to go too fast though, or you will cut straight through the fabric as well as the stitches!

Getting heavy

Denim is pretty tough and can be difficult to sew, so give yourself the best chance by using the appropriate equipment, namely heavy-gauge denim machine needles, which you'll need to change as soon as they seem blunt. Use a long machine stitch and sew slowly and carefully, especially on hems where there are several layers of fabric. Don't try to sew backwards and forwards at the start and end of seams, as you may bend or even snap the needle. Instead, pull the top thread through to the back of the fabric and tie the ends tightly.

Happy bleaching

I use household bleach when I'm decorating denim. I always work outdoors and cover the work surface with a tarpaulin and layers of newspaper. I protect my hands with thick, rubber-covered gloves (you can get these from most hardware stores) and my eyes with safety glasses. I also wear overalls, as bleach splashes can burn straight through fabric.

Use old paintbrushes that you don't mind throwing away afterwards to apply the bleach, because it will eventually rot the bristles.

Patch Perfect

This is a nifty trick for covering up a large tear or worn patch on your jeans. Look out for cool embroidered details on denim clothes, like these appliqué panels I rescued from my daughter's old jeans – they make great patches.

1. Roughly cut out the embroidered panels and apply fusible webbing to the back of each panel following the manufacturer's instructions.

2. Remove the backing paper from the panels, position on your jeans and iron on. Machine stitch around the edges of the patches with zigzag stitch to secure them firmly.

3. Use high-tack fabric glue to attach gemstones and sequins to the patches as embellishment. Add more around the lower edge and outside seam of each leg.

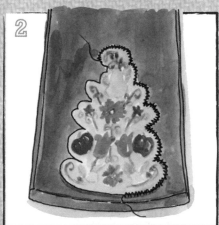

Fab Flares

This is a great way to salvage a pair of too-narrow jeans. Mine were a great fit in every other respect, but I decided that they needed a bit of a flare below the knee. I added fabric at both sides, from a printed silk scarf, and a spotty corsage trim.

1 Decide how long you want your flare to be. Use the seam ripper to open the outside seam of your jeans to this length, plus a 1.5cm (⅝in) seam allowance at the top. Unpick the leg hems and press them flat.

2 Cut your scarf in half lengthways, then fold each half over and press. On each piece, draw a triangle 10cm (4in) wide at the lower edge and 5cm (2in) wide at the top, and the same length as the height of your flare, plus 1.5cm (⅝in) at top and bottom for turnings. Cut out.

* Pair of straight-leg jeans
* Ruler and pen
* Seam ripper
* Iron
* Silk scarf and matching thread
* Scissors
* Pins
* Sewing machine
* Contrasting fabric and matching thread
* Pair of compasses
* Pinking shears
* Hand sewing needle

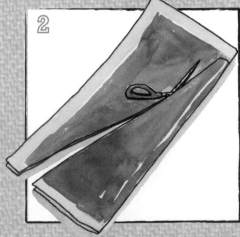

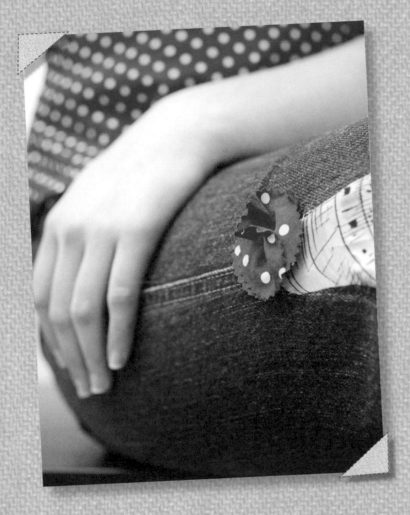

3 Open out and press the triangles flat. Pin one to the side seam of each leg, with right sides together, and machine stitch. Turn the jeans inside out and pin the other side of the triangles to the remaining leg seam, then machine stitch.

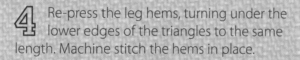

4 Re-press the leg hems, turning under the lower edges of the triangles to the same length. Machine stitch the hems in place.

5 For each corsage, cut three 5cm- (2in-) diameter circles of contrasting fabric. Use pinking shears to make zigzag edges. Fold the two circles for each corsage into quarters and hand sew the point of each one to keep the folds in place. Sew the two folded circles to the third flat circle to complete each corsage, then sew in place at the top of each flare as a trim.

Studs 'n' Spatters

I undid the hem of my daughter's denim skirt because I was going to add a band of contrasting fabric to lengthen it. However, I liked the ragged, beat-up look of the unpicked fabric so much that I decided to leave it and add a trim of star-shaped metal studs instead. For the jacket, I tested the bleach on an innocuous part first to find out how long it took to lift the colour; a couple of minutes will lighten the fabric, and anything up to five minutes will bleach it completely white.

Get it together...

* Denim skirt and matching thread
* Denim jacket
* Ruler and pen
* Star-shaped metal studs
* Hammer
* Sewing machine
* Cotton tape
* Tarpaulin, newspaper and protective clothes
* Household bleach
* Medium-thick artist's paintbrush
* Plastic buckets

Use a ruler and pen to mark the position of the studs along the hem of the skirt. Push the pins of each stud through the fabric where marked. Hammer the pins flat on the back of the fabric. On the back of the skirt, machine stitch a band of cotton tape around the hem of the skirt with matching thread, to cover the backs of the studs.

Before applying bleach to the jacket, stuff the arms with newspaper to stop the bleach from soaking through to the back and marking the fabric. Drip or paint on the bleach with the paintbrush. Bleach will rot the denim if it's left on for too long, so keep an eye on the clock! When happy with the colour, remove the newspaper and dunk the jacket up and down in a plastic bucket of cold water to wash out the excess. Rinse again in a second bucket, then hang up, preferably in the sun, to dry and bleach a little more.

Get more...

» **Are your jeans great in every way except for the length?** Add a **band of contrasting fabric** to extend them to the right length. As long as you pick something made from **natural fibres** that can be washed at the same temperature as your denim, the world's your oyster, so use your imagination and jazz up those jeans!

» **Got a computerized sewing machine?** Chances are it has some pretty nifty embroidery designs in the software. Use this function to create an **embroidered denim patch** to **cover** up **rips** and **thin areas** on your **jeans** (see photo below left). If the rip is quite small, you can embroider directly onto the fabric, which will strengthen the surrounding area too. If you have a large tear or worn area, cut a piece of new denim fabric large enough to cover it, then embroider the denim and stitch over the hole to make a patch.

» As an alternative to embroidered designs, simply thread up your **machine** with **contrasting thread**, set the **stitch length** to **long** and **sew backwards** and **forwards** over the **tear to darn** it. You could also machine stitch a piece of **decorative cotton fabric** over the hole to make a snazzy and **eye-catching patch**.

Check out sari shops and jewellery suppliers for fantastic stick-on gems and metal studs, and keep an eye open for bits of embroidery that you can salvage from other jeans for a cool boho look.

» To give your jeans a fab **distressed** or **faded** appearance:

• **Rub** over the surface with **medium-grade sandpaper**, with a **house brick** or **rough stone** beneath the area you're sanding to provide extra texture; it's easy to rub right through the fabric, so make sure this is the effect you want, or proceed with care!

• If you want to **lighten** your jeans by a **few shades**, soak them in a bucket filled with **one part household bleach** to **three parts water**. Stir the contents at intervals with an old wooden spoon to make sure they bleach evenly, then remove and wash when you're satisfied with the shade.

• **Prefer some precision in your bleached designs?** Draw a **design** onto **oiled Manila stencil card**, then cut it out with a craft knife. Insert a thick layer of newspaper beneath the area you're working on, then attach the **stencil** with masking tape. **Stipple bleach** over the **cutout areas** with a paintbrush, leave to lighten and wash and dry as before.

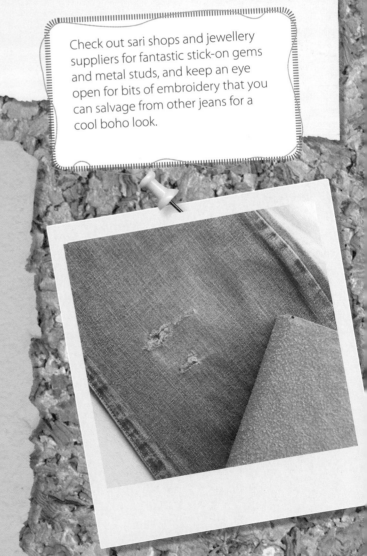

Zippy Fixes

When you're rushing to get dressed, there's nothing more annoying than a stuck zip, and it's all too tempting to give it a sharp tug, which can break it completely. The problem is often a telltale sign that the garment is on the tight side, so inserting a new zip won't resolve things. A row of ribbon eyelets and mismatched buttons or metal eyelets laced up with ribbon or cord provide clever and stylish solutions.

Get into it...

Seize the day...

Think creatively when you're repairing garments. Often you'll find it's the ideal opportunity to re-jig your clothes a bit, especially if they're too large or small. A row of ribbon eyelets is an effective and discreet way of adding give to your garments if they're too tight, and it saves finding a new zip of the right length and inserting it. Don't assume you need buttons to complete the closure – add a row of ribbon eyelets at either side of the opening and simply criss-cross a length of ribbon through to draw the two sides together.

Double measures

If the garment you're repairing is seriously too small for you, consider a double row of buttons, one at either side seam. Make the eyelets as long as you need, because they will look like decorative lacing.

Put on a show

Your eyelets will show up against the fabric of your garment, so make them as subtle or as decorative as you like. You can play around with different colours and combinations of ribbon, then mix and match buttons as you please. Thin cord, tape and round elastic also make good eyelets, so keep a lookout for suitable materials.

Neat fastening

Metal eyelets are a quick and easy way of creating a new fastening. They come in two parts: a post and a collar. The post is inserted through a hole in the fabric, from the back to the front of the garment. Then a small metal collar is snapped or hammered over the top to create the eyelet, sandwiching the raw edges of the hole between to leave a neat finish. A whole row can be created in minutes and then threaded with ribbon, cord or thonging to fasten the opening.

To avoid broken zips in the first place, rub candle wax over the teeth to encourage the pull to glide smoothly without getting jammed. If you do manage to get the zip pull-back onto the teeth, position it about 2cm (¾in) above the end of the zip and make several small stitches below it, to prevent the pull travelling any further.

Hot Metal

Get it together...

* Pair of trousers with broken zip and matching thread
* Seam ripper
* Iron
* Sewing machine
* Metal eyelet kit and hammer
* Narrow ribbon, cord or thonging

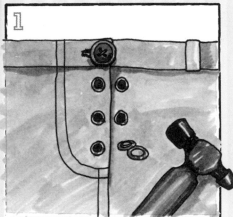

1   Carefully unpick the broken zip from the front of the trousers. Press and restitch the seams. Following the manufacturer's instructions, insert metal eyelets down both halves of the opening, spacing them evenly.

2   Insert a length of narrow ribbon, cord or thonging through the eyelets in a criss-cross pattern to make the fastening.

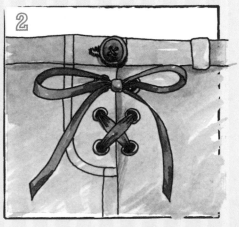

Beautifully Buttoned

1 Carefully unpick the broken zip from the dress seam. Press the side seams flat again, then pin and restitch.

2 To make the ribbon eyelets, cut 10cm (4in) lengths of narrow ribbon. Fold them in half, then press the tops of the loops flat.

Get it together...

* Dress with broken side zip and matching thread
* Seam ripper
* Iron
* Pins
* Sewing machine
* Narrow ribbon in a complementary colour
* Scissors
* Assorted buttons
* Hand sewing needle

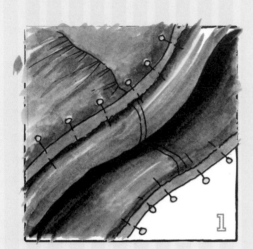

This is a great opportunity to show off your button-covering skills, especially if you've drawn a blank when looking for interesting ready-mades. Simply choose interesting contrasting fabrics and cover-kit buttons of your choice (see the Cool Customizing feature). You can even vary the sizes for a really off-the-wall look.

3 Pin the ribbon eyelets along one half of the opening, spacing them evenly apart. Turn under the raw edges. Machine stitch them in place, sewing close to the turned edge.

4 Pull the sides of the opening together, lining them up as accurately as possible. Sew a button opposite each ribbon eyelet to create the fastening.

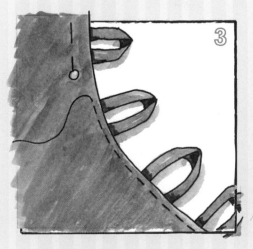

Ribbon Rhythm

1 Carefully unpick the broken zip from the skirt seam. Press the seams flat again, then pin and restitch them.

2 Cut 10cm (4in) lengths of assorted narrow ribbon. Fold the lengths in half, then press the tops of the loops flat. Pin the ribbon eyelets along one half of the opening, then machine stitch them in place, sewing close to the seamed edge. Sew the buttons opposite the ribbon eyelets.

Get it together...

* Skirt with broken zip and matching thread
* Seam ripper
* Iron
* Pins
* Sewing machine
* Assorted narrow ribbon
* Assorted buttons
* Hand sewing needle

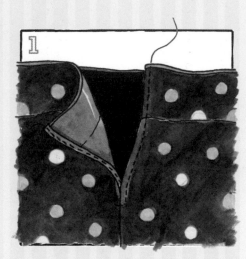

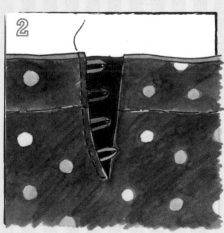

Get more...

» **Don't fancy struggling with a side opening?** Consider **sewing up** the **side seam** permanently, and **repositioning** the opening at the **back** or **front** of your garment instead. This gives you a lot of scope to add **interesting eyelet fastenings** to the **bodice**, or a **cinched-in ribbon fastening** down the **back** of a **skirt**. Just press under and seam the sides of the new opening first, then add **metal** or **ribbon eyelets**.

Like to know more about the salvaging the best bits and bobs to recycle in your makeover projects? See the Perfect Prepping feature.

» **Want another quick and easy way to make a new fastening?** Remove the **buttonhole placket** from an **old shirt**, like the one pictured above, and sew it to **one half** of the **opening**. Line up the edge of the buttonholes with the opening so that they peep out from underneath the turned edge. Sew the **corresponding buttons** to the **other side** of the **opening** to make the fastening. If you want to enlarge an opening, attach the whole placket without unbuttoning it first, then the opening will be increased by the width of the placket in one easy step.

» Don't worry about making discreet fastenings. Use **narrow, decorative ribbon** in lots of **different colours**, plus a handful of **mismatched buttons** for a **cool, boho look**. This is a great way of using up **odds and ends** of **decorative ribbon** and **single buttons** that you've cut off garments to reuse.

» **Don't like eyelets? Hooks and eyes** are a good alternative, and work especially well at the site of an old zip, because there are already two turned edges to sew the fastenings behind. **Oversize press studs** (snap fasteners) also make a style-conscious option. Get the biggest you can find and you may only need two or three to fit the opening.

» **Got a dress with an attached skirt section that has a broken zip?** This presents a good opportunity to transform it into a skirt, rather than replacing the zip with loads of eyelets. Simply unpick and remove the broken zip, then unpick the skirt section from the dress. Press under the raw edge at the top of the skirt to make a narrow hem, then machine stitch it in place. Add ribbon eyelets and buttons at the side opening to make a closure. This produces a low-rise skirt that sits comfortably just below the waistline.

Skirt 'n' Shirt Chic

Here's an easy way to bring summer style to a basic skirt and recycle an old shirt at the same time. I picked up the skirt because I loved the colour and the stitch detail. Then it sat idling until I hit on the idea of a button-thru detail down the front using the button placket from a stripy cotton shirt. The salvaged mismatched pockets add a finishing touch of originality.

Keep it simple

For the best results, choose a skirt with a side fastening. You can use one with a front zip if you particularly like it, but you'll have to unpick and remove the zip, then neaten the edges attractively first. My skirt is very simple, and because there's only one layer of fabric at the waist, it was easy to cut through the front and attach the button placket without creating extra bulk. Pick a straight or A-line, unlined skirt in a medium to heavyweight fabric, such as cotton drill, medium-weight denim or needlecord. The fabric needs to be heavy enough to support the button placket, but not too bulky to sew easily, like when turning over the edges of the waist.

> If possible, choose a skirt without a separate waistband, because it's much easier and neater to alter it.

Perfect the pocket

If your skirt already has pockets, like mine, you could simply attach the new ones on top of the old. Just remember to open out your skirt before stitching to avoid sewing through the back too. My pockets didn't quite stretch across the originals, so I had to lose about 3cm (1¼in) from their width when I sewed the new ones on top. Before I attached them, I lined up the inside edges with the stitched lines to look like an intentional part of the design rather than randomly slapped on. Because the original stitching was so obvious I had to use it in the design, but you can add pockets wherever you like, even along the hemline. Play around with their position, then pin and stitch in place.

Mind the gap

Be aware of the potential extra width created by inserting a piece of fabric such as a shirt placket into the front of a skirt and try to keep this to a minimum. As you trim the placket from the shirt, add a 1.5cm (⅝in) seam allowance to the sides. Line this up with the raw edges of the opened-out skirt front, then stitch close to the placket edges to avoid a gap between the front edges of the skirt.

Keep it buttoned

On no account unbutton the placket before you attach it to the skirt sides. It will be virtually impossible to match the halves once they're undone and your skirt won't hang straight when you rebutton it. It's much easier to sew the placket on while it's buttoned up. Just remember not to stitch through both layers when you press under the top edge, or you won't be able to open it!

1 To find the centre of the skirt, fold it in half and press it flat to make a sharp crease down the front. This is the centre line. Cut carefully down the line on the front of the skirt only, then open it out.

2 Cut the button placket from the front of the shirt. Trim the excess fabric to within 1.5cm (⅝in) of the folded edges of the placket to allow for turnings. Trim the placket top and bottom so that it's the same length as the skirt front, plus 1.5cm (⅝in) at either end for turnings.

Get it together...

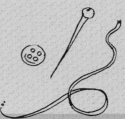

* A-line or straight skirt and matching thread
* Contrasting shirt and matching thread, plus extra salvaged pocket
* Iron
* Scissors
* Sewing machine
* Pins

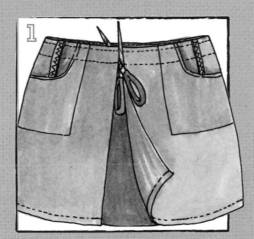

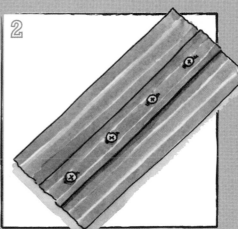

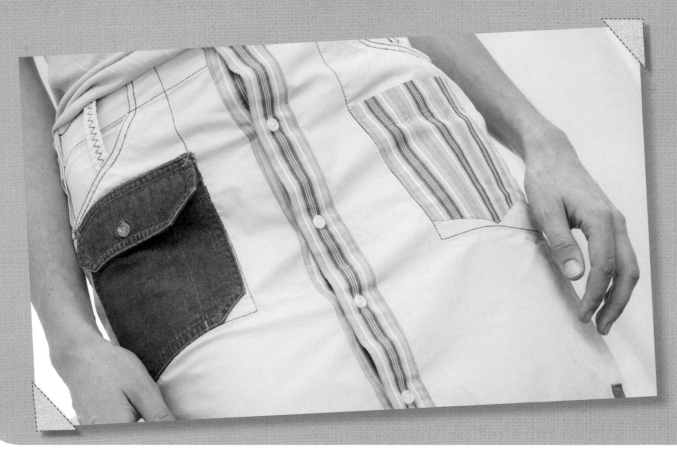

3 Unbutton the top of the placket and press under the top edges by 1.5cm (⅝in) to make turnings. Press under the raw edges and machine stitch them in place to make narrow hems. Repeat to hem the raw edges at the other end of the placket.

4 Without unbuttoning the placket, position one side of it along one front edge of the skirt, with right sides facing. Pin in place, then machine stitch. Repeat to attach the other side of the placket to the other side of the skirt front. Use the overlocking function on your machine if it has one, or a narrow zigzag stitch, along the raw edges at either side to neaten them and prevent fraying.

5 Unpick the pockets you have chosen from their original garments and press them flat. Unbutton the skirt front and pin the pockets in place on either side. Machine stitch them in place, following the original seam lines as you sew.

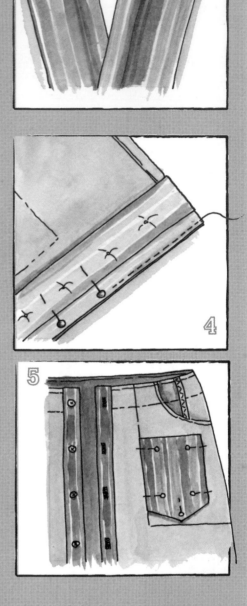

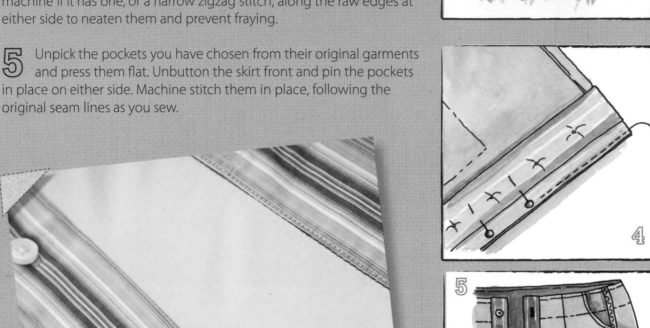

Get more...

» Go for interesting contrasts and textures when choosing skirts and shirts to mix and match. Think:
- **corduroy** with **lightweight woollen suiting**
- **denim** with **satin** or **lace**
- **velvet** with **embroidered fabric**

Button plackets from **denim shirts and jackets** look especially cool when incorporated into a skirt front. **Experiment** with **fabric patterns** and **colours** too.

» **Denim jeans skirts** are also good for this kind of makeover, as long as you can track down one **without a waistband**. If the skirt is front-fastening, simply unpick and remove the zip, then open out the central front seam. Press under and restitch the edges of the seams, then insert a button placket as before. The offset zip cover will look great, so don't worry about trying to hide it by turning under the edges.

» Keep an eye open for **interesting pockets** – they don't need to be shirt pockets like mine were either. And they will look great **anywhere** on your skirt – they don't need to be functional or in a conventional place to work a treat. Try:

- **rows and lines** of pockets

- **randomly** placed **mini** pockets

- an **unusually positioned** pocket in a really **strong contrast** of colour or style like **bright orange wool** on **dark indigo denim**

» With a simple project like this, you can afford to be ultra adventurous, so get out the **sequins**, **buttons** and **ribbons** and add **extra bling** to a basic design. The pockets, especially, are a great empty canvas for a splash of decoration and will look good with anything from **simple embroidery** to iron-on **rhinestone tattoos**.

» **Found an unloved maxi skirt in a fab fabric?** Why not transform it into a minxy little button-thru mini. Simply trim the skirt to the right length, plus 3cm (1¼in) for the hem, before you begin, then proceed as before to insert a button-thru front, adding 3cm (1¼in) to the bottom of the placket rather than 1.5cm (⅝in). Once the buttons are in place, press under the hem allowance and slip stitch in place.

A waistband-free, A-line skirt is a design classic, so if you find one that has seen better days but is practically perfect in every other way, unpick it and draw around the pieces to make a pattern.

GET THE MOST FROM...

Cool CUSTOMIZING

Taking simple clothes and adding special touches to give them a designer finish is fun, and when it comes to customizing your clothes, individuality and creativity are where it's at. For the amount that you'd spend on one new item of clothing, you could revamp your entire wardrobe, creating show-stopping clothes on a tiny budget.

No one wants to go out dressed in exactly the same, boring, high-street outfit as everyone else, and customizing your clothes in a variety of easy and effective ways gives you a cast-iron guarantee that you never will!

Take stock

Like a lot of people, I sometimes look in my wardrobe at rows of clothes and wish I had something to wear. In reality, there's absolutely tons of stuff, but it's just that it all seems a bit tired and uninspiring. The truth is, I've got nothing that I **want** to wear, which is a different thing entirely. On the other hand, I just can't bring myself to part with any of it, even though I haven't worn it in ages, because there's always something about the cut, the cloth or the colour that I still love. So there my too retro, boring, small, stained or torn poor clothes would lie forever, languishing at the back of the wardrobe, if I didn't pull them all out from time to time, reassess their charms and realize how easily they could be revived with a bit of inspired creativity. So do some delving of your own and dig out those candidates for customizing.

Button it

Adding exciting buttons to an outfit can transform its appearance, giving a new and stylish edge to the dullest of garments. So try out these creative buttoning ideas for size:

• Buttons don't need to match – for a fresh look, trawl through your button box to create a set of mismatched buttons in exciting colour combinations. Use them to replace existing buttons on the front of a jacket or cardigan, or stitch them together in clusters at the neckline or wrist to make eye-catching decorations.

• Don't just stick to matching threads to sew on buttons – choose dramatic colour contrasts.

• If your buttons have four buttonholes, experiment with different stitch patterns for extra visual interest – see the examples pictured above.

• If your buttons have very large holes, attach them to your garment with narrow ribbon, leather thonging, string or chenille yarn for a change.

Cover up

Another option is to make your own buttons, either by covering existing ones or by using a button-making kit. This is a great way to use up small scraps of your favourite fabric, especially if they've got interesting motifs, or small areas of embroidery. To cover an existing button:

1 Cut a circle from your desired fabric, about twice as wide as the button you wish to cover.

2 Sew a line of running stitches all round the edge of the fabric, leaving one end loose.

3 Place the button in the centre, then pull the thread up tightly to gather the fabric. Make a few stitches across the edges of the fabric to keep it in place.

Buttons suitable for covering are those that are domed with a shank, rather than flat ones with holes.

Appliqué away

Sometimes I find a garment made from lovely fabric that is just a bit too **LOUD** to wear. However, if the motifs are attractive, I am more than happy to cut them out and appliqué them onto other garments to jazz them up a bit. I find that flora and fauna work best, and a well-placed summer rose or pretty bird can transform a jacket or frock into an ethereal and unique delight.

Keep in trim

One of the quickest ways to transform a plain garment into a thing of beauty is to customize it with some kind of trim. By adding ribbon, tape, lace, braid, sequins, beads or a length of fringeing, you can make it as understated, glam or over the top as you wish. Your trim can even be non-sew, if you tie a length of wide ribbon in a bow or obi-style belt around your waist, or pin it at the neckline of a top or dress. Keep an eye open for excitingly trimmed garments when you're on the lookout in charity shops. You may be able to pick up something with a fantastic trim very cheaply, then simply unpick it and reuse it to pretty up a plain cardi or a pair of jeans.

Precious little

If you've got a jewellery box crammed with old bits and pieces of costume jewellery, now's the time to dust it down and get out your gold:

- **Sparkly brooches** make great **jacket clasps** or **decorations** for the fronts of **party shoes**.
- **Long strings of beads** will add **retro style** to any **dress** if you use them as a **belt**.
- **Shorter necklaces** can be **stitched** around the **neckline and wrists** of a soft **fluffy sweater**.
- **Necklaces** also make great **spaghetti straps** for a glam **party dress** or **top**.
- **Anything spangly** and over the top can be attached to a **handbag** that needs perking up.
- **Bracelets** make great replacement **evening bag handles**.

Artful edging

I do love a three-quarter length sleeve; they're so flattering and elegant. One way to add glamour to an old sweater or cardi is to chop down the sleeves to this length, then add a narrow edging of contrasting patterned fabric. **Plain velvet**, **fake fur** and **feathers** also look lovely, and can add a touch of luxury to a **plain sweater** that's seen better days. You can extend this idea to add **cuffs** to **jackets**, **bands** to **trouser legs** and **jeans** as well as **deep borders** to **long-line jackets** and **coats**.

Stitching pretty

Don't confine your sewing machine to making seams. It's capable of a lot more than that, and a quick flick through the manual it came with will show you all the fancy stitches that it can produce.

- **Zigzag**, **overlock** and **blind hem stitches** are all highly decorative and can be used to great effect to add bands of **machine embroidery** to your garments.

- Use a **bright** or sharply **contrasting coloured thread** to produce a **rustic, hand-smocked look**.

- Sew **closely spaced lines** of **straight stitch** for a **clean**, **understated feel**.

Best cuts

Of course, one of the most effective ways of customizing clothes is simply to cut off the bits you don't like and keep the bits you do, for instance:

- removing sleeves completely
- cutting down a pair of jeans
- removing from or adding pockets to a jacket
- chopping down a maxi skirt into a mini
- transforming a dress into a fab tunic top

You might also want to go down the mix and match route, where you simply take three or more garments and mix them all up, or replace one pair of sleeves with another, combine mismatched fronts and backs or splice two different cardigans together.

GET THE MOST FROM...

Sewing Lounges and SWISHING

In the past few years there's been a huge increase in the popularity of making, upcycling and altering clothes. Some of this is connected to the newly fashionable virtue of thriftiness and a revival of interest in the wartime practice of 'make do and mend'. But there's also a strong desire to live in a greener, more sustainable way and a growing aversion to throwaway clothing, produced cheaply in sweatshops. Mass-market fatigue and the thrill of owning a totally original outfit also play a big part.

I've always been a makeover queen, and now it's really nice to know that I'm not alone. There's loads of like-minded folks out there that are eager to link up and spread the sewing word.

A rose by any other name...

So what is upcycling? There are various takes on the meanings of upcycling and recycling, so I think you'll find it handy if I define what I mean by the different processes:

• **Upcycling** is where an unwanted item is remade to produce an object of greater value. For example, a **baggy old sweater** is upcycled by way of a snazzy makeover into a **bolero cardigan with ruffled trim** – see the Cardi Creative project before and after shots below.

• **Recycling** is where an object is salvaged and remade into another item of lesser value, for example **glass bottles** are crushed to produce **aggregate for road laying**.

Sew go!

If you're new to sewing, a keen improver or just want to get out there and join the scene, then check out your nearest sewing lounge. Here, you can learn the skills you need to make, alter and customize your clothes and groove up your wardrobe. Sewing lounges are drop-in studios that are dedicated to sewing and related subjects such as paper crafts, book binding, soap making and so on. They offer one-off sewing days for enthusiasts of all abilities, where you can learn a particular skill. They also provide structured courses over several sessions, during which you can brush up on the basics, such as getting to grips with commercial sewing patterns, or build on the skills that you already have.

Sewing lounges are great places to celebrate a special event like a birthday or a hen night. It's worth enquiring whether a group of you can visit for a tailor-made, themed sewing session.

Flexible fun

The best thing about sewing lounges is that you can extend your skills in a totally supportive environment and make new friends and contacts at the same time. The courses have a flexible, contemporary approach to creativity (although a wide age range attend) and the emphasis is on learning, sharing experiences and, above all, fun. Forget the image of a stuffy sewing class with rigid rules, strict instructors and uncreative outcomes – sewing lounges are cool!

Sewing Lounges Online

Search the internet to find a lounge in your area; they're popping up all over the UK, USA, Canada and Australia. To whet your appetite, here are three to check out online:

The Make Lounge, in London, England: www.themakelounge.com

Make, in New York City, USA: www.makeworkshop.com

Spool of thread, in Vancouver, Canada: www.spoolofthread.com

Guilt-free trip

We all consume too much, too cheaply, without considering the consequences of our actions. When financial times are hard, it's very tempting to buy ridiculously cheap clothes and throw them away the second they wear out or when we get bored with them. However, this approach can be unethical where clothing manufacturers exploit their workers, and it certainly isn't green. Producing cotton, for example, is very heavy on pesticides, and therefore the planet, so it makes sense to recycle what we already have in abundance in our homes. Many clothing designers have woken up to the reality that they need to produce clothing in a sustainable way, with far less impact on the environment. This is a good start, but when your budget is tight and your head full of ideas, why not cut down waste, save energy and have fun reusing what you've already got?

When you buy new T-shirts, look out for Fair Trade and organic cotton. Many high street manufacturers now sell affordable clothes that tick both these boxes, so you can be sure you're doing your bit to save the planet.

Swap shop

If you're as hooked on clothes as I am, you've probably bought something on the spur of the moment, fallen out of love with it almost immediately, then lived to regret it and cursed the money you've wasted. If so, its time to get acquainted with the swaporama and swishing scenes, and work that wardrobe without spending one single penny more! Swishing parties and swaporamas are the newest, coolest, greenest way to get your hands on fabulous new outfits, while having a lot of fun. What started as an eco-friendly initiative by green PR firm Futerra has become a hot new trend in the UK, USA and Australia, and word is spreading fast – especially via the internet.

• **Swishes** are clothes-swapping parties – fun social events where you can take all your impulse buys and expensive mistakes and then swap them for something you really like instead. Garments, shoes and accessories are all acceptable, as long as they're in good condition, and the more you take, the more you can leave with at the end of the party.

• **Swaporamas** are club and festival-based versions of swishing, where you turn up, hit the dance floor and trade clothes with your nearest neighbour when you hear a signal.

Swap Shops Online

If you can't wait to get started, check out some of the great online swap shops, where you can upload and swap your unwanted clothes once you've registered. Some clothes-swap sites that are worth a look include:

www.bigwardrobe.com
www.posh-swaps.com
www.swapstyle.com
www.mrsbears.co.uk
www.swishing.co.uk

Net gains

You can find lots of information about the ethical issues around clothing manufacture and earth-friendly producers online. There are also some great websites devoted to swishing and swaporamas, with details of upcoming events and tips for hosting your own. Some sites even have party packs with downloadable flyers and e-invites you can mail to friends.

Templates

Top Tees (pages 40–47)

Pocket

Flower

Leaf

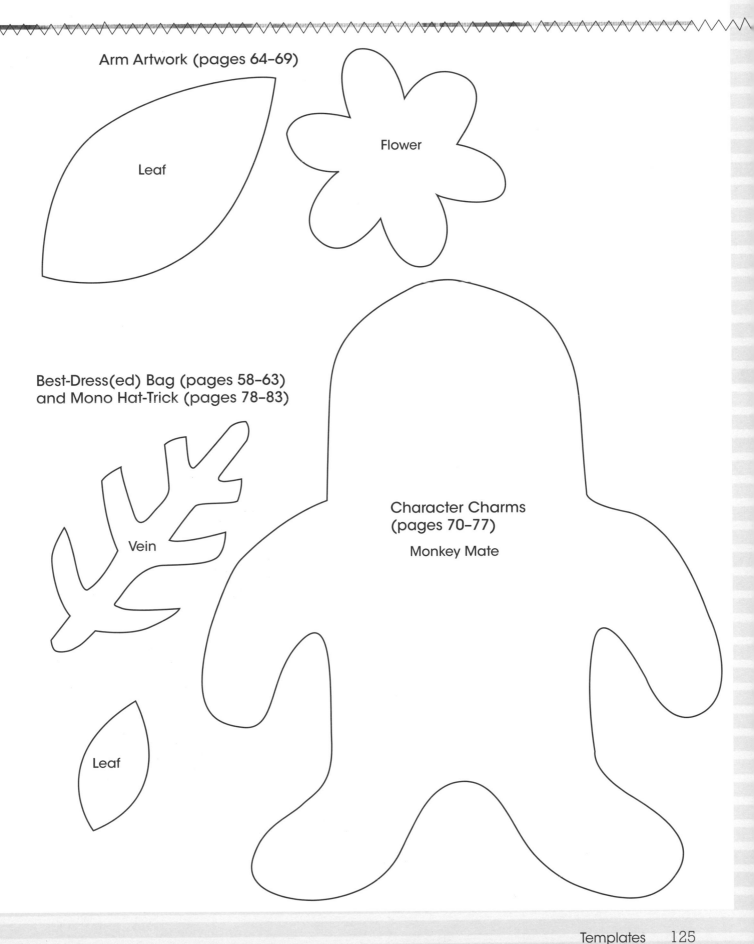

Arm Artwork (pages 64–69)

Leaf

Flower

Best-Dress(ed) Bag (pages 58–63)
and Mono Hat-Trick (pages 78–83)

Vein

Character Charms
(pages 70–77)

Monkey Mate

Leaf

Suppliers

UK

Cancer Research UK
Many shops around the UK, or you can buy vintage from their online shop at:
www.cancerresearch-uk.org.uk

The Make Lounge
49–51 Barnsbury Street
Islington
London N1 1TP
020 7609 0275
www.themakelounge.com

Oxfam
Many shops around the UK, some with dedicated upcycled goods sections, or you can buy vintage from their online shop at:
www.oxfam.org.uk

Pretty Rubbish
www.prettyrubbish.org
Tel: 07970 546 843; 07838 375 023

Sue Ryder Care
Many shops around the UK
114–118 Southampton Row
London WC1B 5AA
Tel: 0845 050 1953
Email: info@suerydercare.org
www.suerydercare.org

US

The Craft Lounge
324 Broad Avenue
Leonia, NJ 07605
(201) 944-3311
info@thecraftlounge.com
www.thecraftlounge.com

The Make Workshop
Design, art and craft classes for kids and adults in New York City
www.makeworkshop.com

Urban Fauna Studios
Fibre art classes in San Francisco, CA
www.urbanfaunastudio.com

About the Author

Marion Elliot is a craft designer and author of more than 20 books, specializing in textile and paper crafts. She lived for many years in London, working as an art director and stylist, before escaping to the wilds of rural Shropshire in England. She now runs her own company, Vintage Town, selling an eclectic range of home accessories such as bags, tea cosies and purses, all made from vintage fabrics that she has collected and scavenged through the years. She has two online shops where you can buy her work, *www.folksy.com/shops/ vintagetown* and *www.etsy.com/shop/ vintagetown* as well as a blog at *www.vintagetown.blogspot.com*

Acknowledgments

I would like, as ever, to thank everyone who has made this book possible. At David and Charles, Jennifer Fox-Proverbs for seeing the potential in careworn clothes, James Brooks for keeping his beady eye on things and Mia Trenoweth for her fab layouts and design. Also, Lorna Yabsley for her great photos, and all the wonderful models. On the home front, Neil and Stella for putting up with piles of clothes, Margaret at the launderette for heavy-duty felting and the staff of all the charity shops in Ludlow, especially the manageress of Cancer Research for allowing me to take photos of her stock. Finally, grateful thanks to copy-editor extraordinaire Jo Richardson for her patience and for calmly pulling it all together once more.

Index